D1356072

COOK smart

Grandma's Recipes

igloobooks

Published in 2015
by Igloo Books Ltd
Cottage Farm
Sywell
NN6 0BJ
www.igloobooks.com

Food photography and recipe development: PhotoCuisine UK
Front and back cover images © PhotoCuisine UK

LEO002 0115
2 4 6 8 10 9 7 5 3 1
ISBN 978-1-78440-163-4

Printed and manufactured in China

Contents

Breakfasts

Baked mushrooms with sausage scramble

Preparation time
10 minutes

Cooking time
30 minutes

Serves 2

Ingredients

2 tbsp butter, melted
4 tbsp wholemeal
  breadcrumbs
1 tbsp Parmesan, finely grated
salt and freshly ground
  black pepper
4 large portabella mushrooms,
  stalks removed
6 large eggs
2 hot dog sausages, sliced
1 tbsp flat leaf parsley,
  chopped

Method

1. Preheat the oven to 200°C (180°C fan) / 390F / gas 6.

2. Mix the butter, breadcrumbs and Parmesan together and season with salt and pepper. Pack the mixture into the mushrooms, then arrange the mushrooms in a baking dish.

3. Bake the mushrooms for 25 minutes or until tender to the point of a knife.

4. Beat the eggs gently in a saucepan and season with salt and pepper. Set the pan over a low heat and stir continuously until they start to scramble.

5. Add the sliced hot dogs and continue to stir until the eggs are cooked to your liking.

6. Serve the mushrooms on hot plates with the eggs spooned onto the side and garnished with parsley.

Smart tip
Don't stop stirring
the egg pan as the
scramble can catch and
burn very easily.

Smart tip

Put the honey pot on
the table so people can
sweeten their porridge
a little more if liked.

Nectarine, blueberry and hazelnut porridge

Preparation time
5 minutes

Cooking time
8 minutes

Serves 4

Ingredients

600 ml / 1 pint / 2 ½ cups
 whole (full-fat) milk, plus
 extra to serve
125 g / 4 ½ oz / 1 ¼ cups
 rolled porridge oats
4 tbsp runny honey
a pinch of salt
1 nectarine, stoned and sliced
100 g / 3 ½ oz / ⅔ cup
 blueberries
3 tbsp toasted hazelnuts
 (cobnuts), chopped

Method

1. Mix the milk with the oats in a saucepan, then stir the mixture over a medium heat until it starts to simmer.

2. Add the honey and a pinch of salt, then reduce the heat to its lowest setting and continue to stir for 4 minutes.

3. Divide the porridge between four bowls and pour over a little extra milk. Top with the nectarine slices, blueberries and hazelnuts.

Cinnamon brioche French toast

Preparation time
4 minutes

Cooking time
4 minutes

Serves 2

Ingredients

2 large eggs
75 ml / 7 ½ fl. oz / ⅓ cup milk
2 tbsp butter
6 thick slices brioche
2 tbsp caster (superfine) sugar
1 tsp ground cinnamon

Method

1. Lightly beat the eggs with the milk in a wide, shallow dish and heat the butter in a large frying pan until sizzling.

2. Dip the brioche slices in the egg mixture on both sides until evenly coated, then fry them in the butter for 2 minutes on each side or until golden brown.

3. Mix the sugar with the cinnamon and sprinkle liberally over the French toast at the table.

Smart tip

Be careful not to over-soak the brioche, as it softens very quickly and may start to dissolve.

Smart tip

The hash browns can be prepared and chilled the night before to save time in the morning.

Full English breakfast

Preparation time
45 minutes

Cooking time
50 minutes

Serves 4

Ingredients

4 tbsp sunflower oil
4 pork sausages
8 rashers smoked back bacon
2 tomatoes, halved
4 mushrooms
400 g / 14 oz / 1 ¾ cups
    canned baked beans
4 large eggs

For the hash browns:
450 g / 1 lb / 1 ½ cups waxy
    potatoes
½ onion, thinly sliced
1 tsp Dijon mustard
1 large egg white
salt and freshly ground
    black pepper
2 tbsp butter

Method

1. To make the hash browns, cook the unpeeled potatoes in boiling water for 18 minutes or until a skewer slides in easily. Drain well, then leave to cool completely before peeling.

2. Coarsely grate the potatoes into a bowl, then stir in the onion. Whisk the mustard into the egg white and season with salt and pepper, then stir it into the potatoes. Shape the mixture into eight triangular patties, then chill for 30 minutes.

3. Melt the butter in a large frying pan then fry the hash browns over a low heat for 15 minutes, turning halfway through. Keep warm in a low oven.

4. Add half of the oil to the frying pan and fry the sausages over a low heat for 15 minutes, turning regularly.

5. While the sausages are cooking, grill the bacon, tomatoes and mushrooms until the bacon is crisp. Bring the beans to a gentle simmer in a small saucepan.

6. When the sausages are ready, transfer them to the oven to keep warm with the hash browns, add the rest of the oil to the frying pan and fry the eggs for 3 minutes or until the whites are set and the yolks are still runny.

7. Divide everything between four warm plates and season with salt and pepper.

Quinoa granola with fromage frais

Preparation time
20 minutes

Cooking time
15 minutes

Serves 4

Ingredients

500 ml / 17 ½ fl. oz / 2 cups
 fromage frais
4 tbsp raspberry jam (jelly)
75 g / 2 ½ oz / ½ cup
 blackberries
75 g / 2 ½ oz / ½ cup
 blueberries
75 g / 2 ½ oz / ½ cup cherries,
 halved and stoned

For the granola:
100 g / 3 ½ oz / ½ cup
 uncooked red and
 white quinoa
2 tbsp flaxseeds
4 tbsp pecan nuts, chopped
2 tbsp agave syrup
¼ tsp ground cinnamon

Method

1. Preheat the oven to 190°C (170°C fan) / 375F / gas 5 and oil a large non-stick baking sheet.

2. Mix all of the granola ingredients together, then spread them out on the baking sheet.

3. Bake for 15 minutes or until golden brown, then remove from the oven and leave to cool for 5 minutes.

4. Scrape the granola pieces onto a plate with a palette knife and leave to cool to room temperature.

5. Divide the fromage frais between four bowls and top with the jam, fruit and granola.

Smart tip

If the granola is cooking
unevenly, give it a stir
halfway through.

Smart tip

Keep an eye on the water so you can start timing as soon as it starts simmering.

Soft-boiled egg and soldiers

Preparation time
5 minutes

Cooking time
4 minutes

Serves 4

Ingredients

4 large eggs
4 slices of white bread

Method

1. Put the eggs in a small saucepan of cold water and bring to a gentle simmer.
2. Cook the eggs for 4 minutes, then drain and transfer to four egg cups.
3. Meanwhile, toast in the bread in a toaster, then cut off and discard the crusts. Cut the toast into thin strips and serve with the eggs.

Fruit salad with strawberry sauce

Preparation time
20 minutes

Serves 4

Ingredients

150 g / 5 ½ oz / 1 cup
  strawberries, hulled
2 tbsp icing (confectioners')
  sugar
½ charantais melon
½ pineapple, peeled and
  cored
1 large banana, sliced
mint sprigs to garnish

Method

1. Purée the strawberries and icing sugar together in a liquidiser to make a smooth sauce.

2. Use a melon baller to scoop the melon into balls. Cut the pineapple into long wedges, then cut them across into slices.

3. Mix the melon balls and pineapple slices with the banana and divide between four bowls. Pour over the strawberry sauce and garnish with mint sprigs.

Smart tip

Taste the sauce before
serving and add a little
extra sugar if it's not
sweet enough.

Smart tip
Try adding some smoked salmon to this omelette for a breakfast treat.

Mushroom and Cheddar omelette

Preparation time
5 minutes

Cooking time
15 minutes

Serves 1

Ingredients

1 tbsp olive oil
4 tbsp butter
75 g / 2 ½ oz / 1 cup button
  mushrooms, sliced
salt and freshly ground
  black pepper
3 large eggs
5 thin slices Cheddar
chervil leaves to garnish

Method

1. Heat the olive oil and half the butter in a large sauté pan until sizzling.

2. Add the mushrooms, season with salt and pepper and cook for 10 minutes, stirring occasionally.

3. Break the eggs into a jug with a pinch of salt and pepper and beat them gently to break up the yolks.

4. Heat the rest of the butter in a non-stick frying pan until sizzling, then pour in the eggs.

5. Cook over a medium heat until the egg starts to set around the outside. Use a spatula to draw the sides of the omelette into the centre and tilt the pan to fill the gaps with more liquid egg.

6. Scatter the mushrooms and Cheddar slices over the top, then continue to cook until the egg is only just set in the centre.

7. Slide the omelette onto a plate and garnish with chervil leaves.

Crumpets

Preparation time
1 hour 15 minutes

Cooking time
45 minutes

Makes 16

Ingredients

225 g / 8 oz / 1 ½ cups strong
white bread flour
225 g / 8 oz / 1 ½ cups plain
(all-purpose) flour
1 tsp baking powder
2 tsp easy-blend yeast
1 ½ tsp fine sea salt
150 ml / 5 ½ fl. oz / ⅔ cup
warm milk
butter to serve

Method

1. Mix all of the dry ingredients together in a bowl. Mix the milk with 500 ml / 16 fl. oz / 2 cups of warm water, then stir it into the dry ingredients to form a thick batter.

2. Cover the bowl with cling film and leave to rise somewhere warm for 1 hour.

3. Oil four metal crumpet ring moulds and sit them in a large non-stick frying pan over a medium heat.

4. Half fill the crumpet rings with the batter and cook for 8 minutes. Use a clean tea towel or tongs to remove the rings, then turn the crumpets over and cook for 2 minutes or until golden brown on top.

5. Transfer the crumpets to a serving plate and repeat three more times or until all of the batter has been used.

6. Serve the crumpets while they're still warm with lashings of butter.

Smart tip

Oil the crumpet rings
well between each
batch to stop them
from sticking.

Smart tip

Weigh out the dry
ingredients and mix
and chill the wet
ingredients the night
before to speed things
up in the morning.

Blueberry pancakes

Preparation time
10 minutes

Cooking time
30 minutes

Serves 4

Ingredients

250 g / 9 oz / 1 ⅔ cups plain (all-purpose) flour
2 tsp baking powder
2 large eggs
300 ml / 10 ½ fl. oz / 1 ¼ cups milk
2 tbsp butter
100 g / 3 ½ oz / ⅔ cup blueberries
maple syrup to serve

Method

1. Mix the flour and baking powder in a bowl and make a well in the centre. Break in the eggs and pour in the milk, then use a whisk to gradually incorporate all of the flour from round the outside to form a batter.

2. Melt the butter in a small frying pan, then whisk it into the batter. Put the buttered frying pan back over a low heat. You will need a tablespoon of batter for each pancake and you should be able to cook four pancakes at a time in the frying pan.

3. Spoon the batter into the pan and cook for 2 minutes or until small bubbles start to appear on the surface of the pancakes.

4. Turn the pancakes over with a spatula and cook the other side until golden brown and cooked through.

5. Repeat until all the batter has been used, keeping the finished batches warm in a low oven.

6. Pile the pancakes onto warm plates, top with blueberries and drizzle with maple syrup.

Eggs Benedict

Preparation time
15 minutes

Cooking time
15 minutes

Serves 4

Ingredients

2 English breakfast muffins, halved
4 large eggs
2 tbsp butter, softened
4 slices prosciutto
1 tbsp chives, finely chopped
freshly ground black pepper

For the hollandaise sauce:
4 tbsp white wine vinegar
1 shallot, finely chopped
1 tsp black peppercorns
1 bay leaf
2 large egg yolks
150 g / 5 ½ oz / ⅔ cup butter, melted

Method

1. To make the hollandaise sauce, put the vinegar, shallot, peppercorns and bay leaf in a small saucepan. Boil until the liquid has reduced by half, then strain it into a mixing bowl.

2. Add the egg yolks and whisk to combine, then set the bowl over a saucepan of simmering water and whisk until pale and thick.

3. Pour the butter into the bowl in a thin stream, whisking all the time, until it has all been incorporated and the sauce is smooth and thick.

4. Turn off the heat under the pan – there will be enough heat in the water to keep the sauce warm while you finish the recipe.

5. Toast the muffin halves and keep warm.

6. Bring a wide saucepan of water to a gentle simmer. Crack each egg into a cup and pour it smoothly into the water, one at a time.

7. Simmer gently for 3 minutes, then remove from the pan with a slotted spoon.

8. Butter the muffin halves and top with the prosciutto slices. Sit a poached egg on top of each one and spoon over the hollandaise. Sprinkle with chives and black pepper and serve immediately.

Smart tip

If it looks like the hollandaise is about to curdle, add 1 tbsp of cold water and whisk until smooth.

Smart tip

These pastries are tricky
and time consuming to
make, but the freshness
and taste are well worth
the effort.

Danish pastries

Preparation time
5 hours

Cooking time
30 minutes

Makes 8

Ingredients

350 g / 12 oz / 2 ⅓ cups strong
  white bread flour
1 tsp easy-blend yeast
2 large eggs, separated
75 ml / 2 ½ fl. oz / ⅓ cup milk
50 ml / 1 ¾ fl. oz / ¼ cup
  double (heavy) cream
2 tbsp caster (superfine) sugar
1 tsp salt
250 g / 9 oz / 1 ¼ cups butter,
  chilled and cubed

For the filling and topping:
2 large egg yolks
50 g / 1 ¾ oz / 1¼ cup caster
  (superfine) sugar
2 tbsp plain (all-purpose) flour
2 tbsp cornflour (cornstarch)
1 tsp almond extract
225 ml / 8 fl. oz / ¾ cup whole
  (full-fat) milk
3 tbsp flaked (slivered) almonds
200 g / 7 oz / 2 cups icing
  (confectioners') sugar
1 lemon, juiced

Method

1. Mix 50 g / 2 oz / ⅓ cup of the flour with the yeast and
    75 ml / 3 fl. oz / ⅓ cup of warm water and leave somewhere
    warm for 1 hour.

2. Whisk the egg yolks with the milk, cream, sugar and salt,
    then slowly incorporate into the yeast mixture. Mix in the
    butter cubes and remaining flour, then knead briefly on a
    floured surface.

3. Roll out the dough, then fold into thirds and roll again.
    Fold the dough into thirds again, then chill for 30 minutes.
    Repeat the rolling, folding and chilling twice more.

4. To make the filling, stir the egg yolks, sugar, flours and
    almond extract together in a saucepan, then gradually add
    the milk.

5. Heat the mixture until it starts to boil, stirring all the time,
    then take off the heat and beat vigorously to remove any
    lumps. Press a sheet of cling film onto the surface and leave
    to cool to room temperature.

6. Roll out the dough and cut it into eight squares. Top each
    square with a heaped tablespoon of the filling and sprinkle
    with almonds. Fold the four corners in, then turn the eight
    new corners you've just made in too.

7. Transfer the pastries to a lined baking tray, cover with oiled
    cling film and leave to rise for 1 hour or until doubled in size.

8. Preheat the oven to 200°C (180°C fan) / 400F / gas 6.

9. Bake for 30 minutes, reducing the heat to 180°C (160°C fan)
    / 350F / gas 4 after the first 10 minutes.

10. Sieve the icing sugar into a bowl, then add just enough
    lemon juice to make a thick icing. Leave the pastries to cool
    for 15 minutes, then drizzle over the icing before serving.

Hash browns with egg and bacon

Preparation time
1 hour 15 minutes

Cooking time
35 minutes

Serves 4

Ingredients

450 g / 1 lb / 1 ½ cups waxy
   potatoes
2 tbsp butter, melted
4 tbsp double (heavy) cream
50 g / 1 ¾ oz / ½ cup Cheddar,
   grated
salt and freshly ground
   black pepper
4 large eggs
4 rashers bacon, sliced

Method

1. Cook the unpeeled potatoes in boiling water for 18 minutes or until a skewer slides in easily. Drain well, then leave to cool completely before peeling.

2. Preheat the oven to 190°C (170°C fan) / 375F / gas 5.

3. Coarsely grate the potatoes, then stir in the butter, cream and cheese and season with salt and pepper.

4. Divide the potato mixture between four individual baking dishes and make a slight hollow in the centres. Break an egg into each one and sprinkle over the sliced bacon.

5. Transfer the dishes to the oven and bake for 15 minutes or until the egg whites have set, but the yolks are still a little runny. Serve immediately.

Smart tip

If the potato mixture looks a little dry, stir in a bit more cream.

Smart tip

Make sure your
bananas are very ripe
for the best results.

Banana and poppy seed muffins

Preparation time
15 minutes

Cooking time
18 minutes

Makes 12

Ingredients

3 bananas
100 g / 3 ½ oz / ½ cup soft
    light brown sugar
2 large eggs
125 ml / 4 ½ fl. oz / ½ cup
    sunflower oil
2 tbsp poppy seeds
225 g / 8 oz / 1 ½ cups plain
    (all-purpose) flour
1 tsp bicarbonate of
    (baking) soda

Method

1. Preheat the oven to 200°C (180°C fan) / 400F / gas 6 and line a 12-hole cupcake tin with greaseproof paper squares.

2. Mash the bananas with a fork, then whisk in the sugar, eggs, oil and poppy seeds.

3. Sieve the flour and bicarbonate of soda into the bowl and stir just enough to evenly mix all the ingredients together.

4. Divide the mixture between the paper cases, then transfer the tin to the oven and bake for 18 minutes. Test with a wooden toothpick, if it comes out clean, the cakes are done.

5. Transfer the cakes to a wire rack and leave to cool a little before serving.

Soups and Salads

Tomato and thyme soup

Preparation time
5 minutes

Cooking time
30 minutes

Serves 4

Ingredients

2 tbsp olive oil
1 onion, finely chopped
4 cloves of garlic, crushed
2 tbsp thyme leaves
450 g / 1 lb / 3 cups ripe
  tomatoes, diced
500 ml / 17 ½ fl. oz / 2 cups
  vegetable stock
salt and freshly ground
  black pepper

Method

1. Heat the oil in a saucepan and fry the onion for 8 minutes or
    until softened.

2. Add the garlic and half of the thyme to the pan and cook
    for 2 more minutes, then stir in the tomatoes and vegetable
    stock and bring to the boil.

3. Simmer for 20 minutes, then blend until smooth with a
    liquidiser or stick blender.

4. Taste the soup and adjust the seasoning with salt and
    pepper, then ladle into bowls and sprinkle with the rest
    of the thyme.

Smart tip

There's no need to
skin or deseed the
tomatoes as the soup
is liquidised.

Smart tip
Use an orange-fleshed
sweet potato rather
than one with a white
flesh for a vibrant look.

Sweet potato and carrot soup

Preparation time
10 minutes

Cooking time
30 minutes

Serves 6

Ingredients

2 tbsp butter

6 spring onions (scallions), chopped

2 cloves of garlic, finely chopped

1 tsp ground coriander (cilantro)

1 large sweet potato, peeled and cubed

2 large carrots, peeled and cubed

1 litre / 1 pint 15 fl. oz / 4 cups vegetable stock

2 tbsp coriander (cilantro) leaves

Method

1. Heat the butter in a large saucepan and gently fry the spring onions and garlic for 5 minutes to soften.

2. Add the coriander, sweet potato and carrots to the pan and stir to coat in the butter, then pour in the stock and bring to the boil. Reduce the heat a little and simmer for 20 minutes or until the vegetables are tender.

3. Blend the soup until smooth, using a liquidiser or stick blender, then taste and adjust the seasoning.

4. Ladle into bowls and garnish with coriander leaves.

Chilled courgette, mint and feta soup

Preparation time
10 minutes

Cooking time
20 minutes

Chilling time
2 hours

Serves 6

Ingredients

2 tbsp olive oil
1 onion, finely chopped
2 cloves of garlic, finely
  chopped
4 courgettes (zucchinis),
  chopped
1 litre / 1 pint 15 fl. oz / 4 cups
  vegetable stock
3 tbsp mint leaves, shredded
100 g / 3 ½ oz / ¼ cup feta,
  crumbled
salt and freshly ground
  black pepper

Method

1. Heat the oil in a large saucepan, then fry the onion, garlic and courgettes for 10 minutes, stirring occasionally.

2. Pour in the vegetable stock and bring to the boil, then simmer for 10 minutes.

3. Stir in half of the mint and feta, then season to taste with salt and pepper. Transfer the soup to a liquidiser and blend until smooth.

4. Leave the soup to cool to room temperature, then chill for 2 hours.

5. Ladle the soup into chilled bowls and garnish with the rest of the mint and feta.

Smart tip

Taste the soup for seasoning again just before serving – cold food often needs a little more than hot food.

Smart tip

If the soup is too thick, thin it with a little more vegetable stock or water.

Carrot, lentil and coconut soup

Preparation time
10 minutes

Cooking time
40 minutes

Serves 6

Ingredients

3 tbsp vegetable oil
1 onion, finely chopped
2 tsp fresh root ginger, finely chopped
2 cloves of garlic, crushed
2 large carrots, peeled and sliced
200 g / 7 oz / 1 ⅓ cups red lentils
1 litre / 1 pint 15 fl. oz / 4 cups vegetable stock
200 ml / 7 fl. oz / ¾ cup coconut milk
2 tbsp desiccated coconut

Method

1. Heat the oil in a saucepan and fry the onion and ginger for 5 minutes or until softened.

2. Add the garlic and carrots to the pan and cook for 2 minutes, then stir in the lentils and cook for 1 more minute.

3. Pour in the stock and coconut milk and bring to the boil, then reduce the heat a little and simmer for 30 minutes or until the lentils are tender.

4. Ladle two thirds of the soup into a liquidiser and blend until smooth, then stir it back into the saucepan and season to taste with salt.

5. Divide the soup between six warm bowls and garnish with desiccated coconut.

Watercress and mushroom soup

Preparation time
10 minutes

Cooking time
15 minutes

Serves 4

Ingredients

2 tbsp olive oil
2 tbsp butter
1 small onion, chopped
2 cloves of garlic, crushed
150 g / 5 ½ oz / 2 cups
   mushrooms, chopped
1 litre / 1 pint 15 fl. oz / 4 cups
   vegetable stock
200 g / 7 oz / 6 cups
   watercress, washed and
   chopped
salt and freshly ground
   black pepper
2 tbsp chervil, chopped

Method

1. Heat the oil and butter in a saucepan and fry the onion for 5 minutes or until softened. Add the garlic and mushrooms to the pan and fry for a further 5 minutes, stirring regularly.

2. Pour in the vegetable stock and bring to the boil, then simmer for 5 minutes.

3. Stir in the watercress, then transfer half of the soup to a liquidiser and blend until smooth. Stir the blended soup back into the saucepan and season to taste with salt and pepper.

4. Ladle the soup into bowls and garnish with chervil.

Smart tip

Adding the watercress right at the end helps to retain its nutrients.

Smart tip

You can use any combination of root vegetables to make this soup – just cook until tender.

Root vegetable soup

Preparation time
5 minutes

Cooking time
35 minutes

Serves 6

Ingredients

2 tbsp olive oil
2 tbsp butter
1 onion, finely chopped
2 cloves of garlic, crushed
1 large carrot, peeled
    and diced
2 celery sticks, diced
1 parsnip, peeled and diced
¼ swede, peeled and diced
1 litre / 1 pint 15 fl. oz / 4 cups
    vegetable stock
4 tbsp double (heavy) cream
salt and freshly ground
    black pepper

Method

1. Heat the oil and butter in a saucepan and fry the onion for
    5 minutes or until softened.

2. Add the garlic and vegetables to the pan and sauté for
    5 more minutes, then stir in the stock and bring to the boil.

3. Simmer for 25 minutes or until the vegetables are very
    tender. Ladle the soup into a liquidiser with the cream and
    blend until smooth.

4. Season to taste with salt and pepper, then pour the soup
    into bowls and serve.

Creamy chicken and vegetable soup

Preparation time
5 minutes

Cooking time
15 minutes

Serves 4

Ingredients

2 tbsp butter
1 leek, sliced
1 carrot, peeled and julienned
600 ml / 1 pint / 2 ½ cups
  chicken stock
8 asparagus spears, cut into
  short lengths
450 g / 1 lb / 1 ¾ cups skinless
  chicken breast, sliced
100 g / 3 ½ oz / ⅔ cup peas,
  defrosted if frozen
300 ml / 10 ½ fl. oz / 1 ¼ cups
  double (heavy) cream
salt and white pepper
chervil leaves to garnish

Method

1. Heat the butter in a saucepan and sauté the leek and carrot for 5 minutes without browning.

2. Pour in the stock and add the asparagus and chicken and simmer for 5 minutes.

3. Add the peas and cream and simmer for a further 5 minutes then taste for seasoning and add salt and white pepper as necessary. Serve garnished with chervil leaves.

Smart tip

You can also use leftover roast chicken to make this soup – add it at the same time as the peas.

Smart tip

Traditionally, the baguette slices are topped with rouille and sprinkled with cheese before being added to the soup.

Fish soup

Preparation time
25 minutes

Cooking time
35 minutes

Serves 4

Ingredients

2 tbsp olive oil
1 onion, finely chopped
½ fennel bulb, finely chopped
3 cloves of garlic, crushed
2 tbsp tomato purée
2 tbsp aniseed liqueur
450 g / 1 lb / 1 ¾ cups small
    mixed whole fish
1 litre / 1 pint 15 fl. oz / 4 cups
    fish stock
2 tbsp parsley, chopped
stale baguette slices and
    grated Emmental to serve

For the rouille:
1 chargrilled red pepper,
    peeled
3 cloves of garlic, crushed
½ tsp smoked paprika
2 tbsp fresh white
    breadcrumbs
175 ml / 6 fl. oz / ⅔ cup
    olive oil
salt and freshly ground
    black pepper

Method

1. Heat the oil in a saucepan and fry the onion and fennel
    for 10 minutes or until softened. Add the garlic and cook
    for 2 more minutes, then stir in the tomato purée and
    aniseed liqueur.

2. Add the fish to the pan, then pour in the stock and bring to a
    simmer. Simmer for 20 minutes or until the fish are very soft.

3. While the soup is cooking, make the rouille. Put the pepper,
    garlic, paprika and breadcrumbs in a mini food processor.
    Blend until smooth, then add the olive oil in a thin trickle
    with the blades still running to make a mayonnaise-like
    consistency. Season to taste with salt and pepper.

4. When the soup is ready, transfer it to a liquidiser and blend
    until very smooth. Season to taste with salt and pepper.

5. Pour the soup into bowls and garnish with parsley. Serve
    with stale baguette slices, grated Emmental and the rouille.

Oxtail, beetroot and barley soup

Preparation time
15 minutes

Cooking time
2 hours 50 minutes

Serves 4

Ingredients

2 tbsp olive oil
1 onion, chopped
1 carrot, peeled and sliced
3 medium beetroots,
    peeled and cubed
150 g / 5 ½ oz / ¾ cup
    pearl barley
4 oxtail cutlets
¼ savoy cabbage, cubed
salt and freshly ground
    black pepper

Method

1. Heat the oil in a large saucepan and gently fry the onion,
    carrot and beetroot for 5 minutes. Stir in the barley, then
    add the oxtail and pour over 1.5 litres / 3 pints / 6 cups of
    boiling water.

2. Turn the heat down, partially cover the pan and simmer the
    soup for 2 hours 30 minutes.

3. Remove the oxtail from the pan and add the cabbage, then
    simmer for a further 15 minutes.

4. Meanwhile, shred the meat off the bones. Discard the bones
    and return the meat to the soup, then season to taste with
    salt and pepper.

Smart tip

Oxtail is a good-value cut of meat that makes delicious stock for soups.

Cheesy pea and ham soup

Preparation time
10 minutes

Cooking time
15 minutes

Serves 4

Ingredients

2 tbsp olive oil
2 tbsp butter
1 onion, finely chopped
2 garlic cloves, crushed
400 g / 14 oz / 2 ⅔ cups peas,
    defrosted if frozen
1 litre / 1 pint 15 fl. oz / 4 cups
    ham stock
100 g / 3 ½ oz / ½ cup
    cream cheese
salt and freshly ground
    black pepper
4 rashers smoked streaky
    bacon, halved
2 tbsp Cheddar, grated

Method

1. Heat the oil and butter in a saucepan and fry the onion for
   5 minutes or until softened.

2. Add the garlic and peas to the pan and cook for 2 more
   minutes, then stir in the stock and bring to the boil.

3. Simmer for 5 minutes then stir in the cream cheese.
   Blend the soup until smooth with a liquidiser or stick
   blender, then try the soup and adjust the seasoning with
   salt and pepper.

4. Cook the bacon under a hot grill until crisp. Pour the soup
   into mugs or bowls and garnish with bacon and a sprinkle
   of cheese.

French onion soup

Preparation time
5 minutes

Cooking time
40 minutes

Serves 6

Ingredients

2 tbsp olive oil
3 large onions, chopped
2 garlic cloves, crushed
1 litre / 1 pint 14 fl. oz / 4 cups
    vegetable stock
salt and freshly ground
    black pepper

For the cheese toasts:
4 slices of baguette
50 g / 1 ¾ oz / ½ cup
    Gruyère, grated

Method

1. Heat the oil in a saucepan then add the onions and stir
    well. Cover the pan and cook gently for 20 minutes, stirring
    occasionally. Add the garlic and cook uncovered for 2 more
    minutes, then stir in the vegetable stock and bring to
    the boil.

2. Simmer for 15 minutes, then taste the soup and adjust the
    seasoning with salt and pepper.

3. Meanwhile, toast the baguette slices on one side under a
    hot grill. Turn them over and top with the cheese, then cook
    until golden brown and bubbling.

4. When the soup is ready, pour half of it into a liquidiser and
    blend until smooth. Stir the blended soup back into the pan.

5. Ladle the soup into bowls and float the cheese toasts on top.

Smart tip
Adding the garlic
after the onions have
cooked reduces the risk
of it burning.

Smart tip
This recipe can also be made with smoked cod or pollock.

Smoked haddock chowder

Preparation time
15 minutes

Cooking time
40 minutes

Serves 4

Ingredients

1 litre / 1 pint 15 fl. oz /
   4 cups milk
300 g / 10 ½ oz / 1 ¼ cups
   smoked haddock fillet
2 tbsp olive oil
2 tbsp butter
3 leeks, halved and
   thickly sliced
2 cloves of garlic, crushed
3 medium potatoes, peeled
   and julienned
salt and freshly ground
   black pepper
2 tbsp chives, chopped

Method

1. Heat the milk in a saucepan until it starts to simmer, then add the haddock. Simmer gently for 5 minutes, then turn off the heat and leave for a further 5 minutes. Remove the haddock from the pan with a slotted spoon and reserve.

2. Heat the oil and butter in a separate saucepan and fry the leeks for 8 minutes or until softened.

3. Add the garlic and potatoes to the pan and cook for 2 more minutes, then stir in the milk from the haddock and bring to the boil.

4. Simmer for 20 minutes then transfer the soup to a liquidiser and blend until smooth.

5. Pour the soup back into the saucepan and heat gently. Flake the haddock, discarding the skin and bones, and stir it into the soup. Taste and adjust the seasoning with salt and pepper.

6. Ladle the soup into bowls and garnish with chives.

Pumpkin soup with Parmesan tuiles

Preparation time
15 minutes

Cooking time
40 minutes

Serves 6

Ingredients

2 tbsp butter
1 onion, chopped
2 cloves of garlic, crushed
1 small culinary pumpkin,
    peeled, seeded and cubed
1 litre / 1 pint 14 fl. oz / 4 cups
    vegetable stock
4 tbsp double (heavy) cream
salt and freshly ground
    black pepper
3 tbsp Parmesan, grated
1 tbsp poppy seeds

For the Parmesan tuiles:
50 g / 1 ¾ oz / ½ cup
    Parmesan, grated
2 tbsp poppy seeds

Method

1. Heat the butter in a saucepan and fry the onion for 5 minutes or until softened.

2. Add the garlic to the pan and cook for 2 more minutes, then add the pumpkin.

3. Pour in the stock and simmer for 25 minutes or until the pumpkin is tender.

4. Meanwhile, preheat the oven to 180°C (160°C fan) / 350F / gas 4.

5. To make the tuiles, mix the Parmesan with the poppy seeds, then use a round cookie cutter to shape the mixture into 6 circles on a non-stick baking tray.

6. Transfer the tray to the oven and cook for 3 minutes or until the cheese has melted. Leave to cool and harden on the tray for a few minutes, then lift off with a palette knife.

7. Blend the soup in a liquidiser with the cream until smooth, then taste for seasoning, adding salt and pepper as necessary.

8. Ladle the soup into bowls and sprinkle with Parmesan and poppy seeds. Serve with the tuiles.

Smart tip
Use a sharp paring knife to peel the pumpkin if it's too tough for a peeler.

Smart tip
You can also use vacuum-packed chestnuts for this recipe.

Chestnut and chickpea soup

Preparation time
15 minutes

Cooking time
25 minutes

Serves 6

Ingredients

3 tbsp vegetable oil
1 onion, finely chopped
4 cloves of garlic, finely
chopped
1 large potato, peeled and
diced
1 large carrot, peeled and
diced
400 g / 14 oz / 2 cups canned
chickpeas (garbanzo
beans), drained
200 g / 7 oz / 1 cup canned
chestnuts, drained
1.2 litres / 2 pints / 4 ¾ cups
vegetable stock
salt and freshly ground
black pepper
50 g / 1 ¾ oz piece of
Parmesan

Method

1. Heat the oil in a large saucepan and gently fry the onion and
   garlic for 5 minutes.

2. Stir in the potato, carrot, chickpeas and chestnuts, then pour
   in the stock. Simmer for 20 minutes.

3. Ladle half of the soup into a liquidiser and blend until
   smooth, then stir the blended soup back into the pan.
   Season to taste with salt and pepper.

4. Ladle the soup into bowls and use a vegetable peeler to
   shave over the Parmesan.

Tomato and mozzarella salad with sprouting seeds

Preparation time
10 minutes

Serves 4

Ingredients

4 large ripe tomatoes
2 mozzarella balls
2 tbsp balsamic vinegar
4 tbsp olive oil
salt and freshly ground
    black pepper
2 tbsp basil leaves, shredded
1 tbsp baby capers, chopped
100 g / 3 ½ oz / ⅔ cup mixed
    sprouting seeds

Method

1. Cut the tomatoes in half, then slice them across into half-moons.

2. Slice the mozzarella, then arrange on four plates with the tomatoes.

3. Whisk the vinegar and oil together, then season with salt and pepper and stir in the basil and capers.

4. Spoon the dressing over the tomatoes and mozzarella, then add a small pile of sprouting seeds to the centre of each one.

Smart tip

Use the best quality buffalo mozzarella you can find.

Rice salad Niçoise

Preparation time
20 minutes

Cooking time
20 minutes

Serves 4

Ingredients

200 g / 7 oz / 1 cup long
    grain rice
4 large eggs
75 g / 2 ½ oz / ½ cup green
    beans, cut into short lengths
½ white onion, quartered
    and sliced
75 g / 2 ½ oz / ½ cup canned
    tuna, drained and flaked
12 cherry tomatoes, halved
50 g / 1 ¾ oz / ⅓ cup
    Niçoise olives
50 g / 1 ¾ oz / 2 cups baby
    spinach leaves

For the dressing:
1 clove of garlic, crushed
2 tsp Dijon mustard
1 tsp caster (superfine) sugar
1 lemon, juiced
5 tbsp olive oil
salt and freshly ground
    black pepper

Method

1. Put the rice in a saucepan and add enough water to cover it by 1 cm (½ in). Bring the pan to the boil, then cover and turn down the heat to its lowest setting.

2. Cook for 10 minutes, then turn off the heat and leave to stand, without lifting the lid, for 10 minutes. Spread the rice out on a plate and leave to cool to room temperature.

3. Meanwhile, cook the eggs in boiling water for 6 minutes, then drain well and plunge into cold water.

4. Cook the beans in boiling, salted water for 4 minutes or until cooked al dente. Drain well, then plunge into cold water. Drain again.

5. Peel the eggs and cut them into quarters. Toss with the rice, beans, onion, tuna, cherry tomatoes, olives and spinach.

6. To make the dressing, whisk the garlic, mustard and sugar together, then whisk in the lemon juice. Add the oil in a thin stream, whisking all the time, until emulsified. Season to taste with salt and pepper, then use to dress the salad.

Chickpea, lentil and cabbage salad

Preparation time
10 minutes

Cooking time
20 minutes

Serves 6

Ingredients

3 tbsp olive oil
1 onion, finely chopped
2 cloves of garlic, crushed
½ tsp chilli (chili) flakes
½ tsp ground cumin
400 g / 14 oz / 1 ⅔ cups
    canned chickpeas
    (garbanzo beans), drained
200 g / 7 oz / ¾ cup canned
    lentils, drained
200 g / 7 oz / ¾ cup canned
    tomatoes, chopped
½ savoy cabbage, sliced
salt and freshly ground black
    pepper
lime wedges, pitta bread and
    mint yoghurt to serve

Method

1. Heat the oil in a saucepan and fry the onion and garlic for 5 minutes, stirring occasionally.

2. Stir in the chilli flakes and cumin, then add the chickpeas, lentils and tomatoes. Add a splash of water, then simmer for 15 minutes or until the tomatoes have reduced to a thick sauce.

3. Meanwhile, cook the cabbage in lightly salted, boiling water for 4 minutes or until cooked al dente. Drain well, then plunge into iced water and drain again.

4. When the chickpeas are ready, season to taste with salt and pepper, then leave them to cool to room temperature and toss with the cabbage. Serve with lime wedges for squeezing over and pitta bread and mint yoghurt on the side.

Smart tip

To make the mint yoghurt, combine chopped mint and Greek yoghurt with a squeeze of lemon and a spoonful of honey.

Smart tip
Use a mandolin to slice the vegetables for an even finish.

Chicken, apple and red cabbage salad

Preparation time
20 minutes

Cooking time
6 minutes

Serves 4

Ingredients

4 skinless chicken breasts, sliced
3 tbsp olive oil
salt and freshly ground black pepper
1 red apple
½ lemon, juiced
¼ red cabbage, shredded
½ red onion, thinly sliced
100 g / 3 ½ oz / ⅔ cup radishes, thinly sliced
75 g / 2 ½ oz / 3 cups lamb's lettuce

For the dressing:
2 tsp runny honey
1 lemon, juiced
a pinch of salt
4 tbsp olive oil
2 tbsp chives, chopped

Method

1. Brush the chicken with oil and season well with salt and pepper.

2. Heat a griddle pan until smoking hot, then griddle the chicken slices for 3 minutes on each side or until cooked through.

3. Cut the apple into thin slices then toss with the lemon juice to stop it going brown. Toss the chicken and apple with the cabbage, onion, radishes and lettuce.

4. To make the dressing, whisk the honey and lemon juice with a big pinch of salt, then gradually incorporate the oil. Stir in the chives, then toss with the salad and serve.

Veal Caesar salad

Preparation time
15 minutes

Cooking time
15 minutes

Serves 4

Ingredients

2 thick slices white bread
4 tbsp olive oil
1 large rose veal steak
salt and freshly ground
    black pepper
50 g / 1 ¾ oz piece of
    Parmesan
1 cos lettuce, sliced
1 head of red chicory
    (endive), sliced

For the dressing:
2 tbsp mayonnaise
½ garlic clove, crushed
1 anchovy fillet, finely
    chopped
1 tbsp Parmesan, finely grated
½ lemon, juiced
2 tbsp olive oil

Method

1. Preheat the oven to 190°C (170°C fan) / 375F / gas 5.

2. To make the dressing, mix the mayonnaise with the garlic, chopped anchovy and grated Parmesan, then use a fork to whisk in the lemon juice and olive oil.

3. Cut off and discard the crusts from the bread, then brush the slices with oil on both sides. Tear the bread into chunks and spread them out on a baking tray. Bake the croutons in the oven for 6 minutes or until crisp and golden. Transfer to a wire rack to cool.

4. While the croutons are cooking, heat a griddle pan until smoking hot. Season the veal liberally with salt and black pepper, then griddle for 4 minutes on each side or until cooked to your liking. Leave the steak to rest while you assemble the rest of the ingredients.

5. Use a vegetable peeler to shave the Parmesan into thin slices and arrange on four serving plates with the salad leaves and croutons.

6. Cut the veal into slices and serve on top of the salad with the dressing on the side for spooning over.

Smart tip

The veal steak can be
replaced with chicken
breast or rashers of
streaky bacon.

Smart tip

Try to keep the diced vegetables all the same size for the best presentation.

Greek salad

Preparation time
25 minutes

Serves 4

Ingredients

2 large tomatoes, diced

1 green pepper, deseeded
    and diced

½ cucumber, peeled and
    diced

1 white onion, peeled and
    chopped

100 g / 3 ½ oz / ⅔ cup feta,
    diced

100 g / 3 ½ oz / ⅔ cup black
    olives in oil, drained

½ tsp dried oregano

1 lemon, juiced

4 tbsp olive oil

salt and freshly ground
    black pepper

Method

1. Combine all of the ingredients and leave to marinate
   for 20 minutes.

2. Divide between four plates, season with salt and pepper
   and serve.

Courgette, ham and mini mozzarella salad

Preparation time
10 minutes

Serves 4

Ingredients

1 medium courgette (zucchini)
salt and freshly ground black
   pepper
2 medium tomatoes,
   cut into wedges
300 g / 10 ½ oz / 2 cups mini
   mozzarella balls, drained
2 slices cooked ham, julienned
a large handful of rocket
   (arugula) leaves
2 tbsp toasted pine nuts
1 tbsp basil leaves, shredded
1 tbsp young thyme leaves

Method

1. Cut the courgette into long ribbons with a vegetable peeler and season with salt and pepper.

2. Toss with the tomatoes, mozzarella, ham and rocket and divide between four bowls.

3. Sprinkle over the pine nuts, shredded basil and thyme leaves and serve immediately.

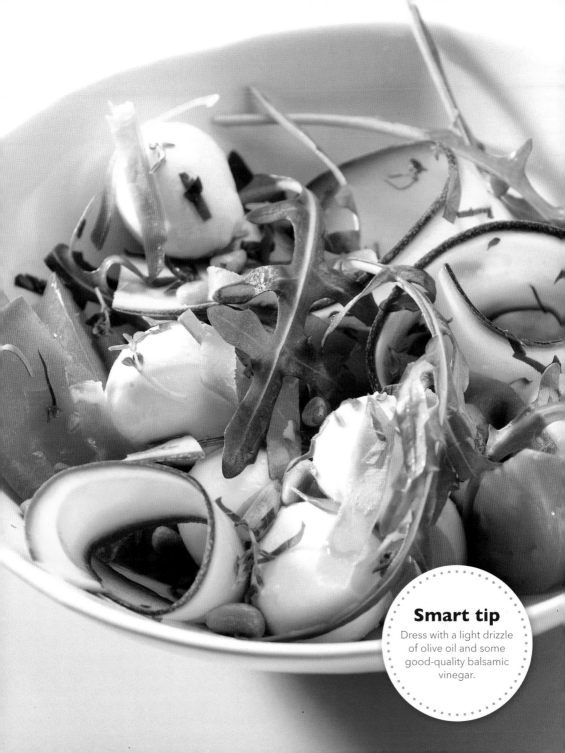

Smart tip

Dress with a light drizzle of olive oil and some good-quality balsamic vinegar.

Main Meals

Roast chicken with new potatoes and garlic

Preparation time
10 minutes

Cooking time
1 hour 20 minutes

Serves 4

Ingredients

800 g / 1 lb 12 oz / 4 cups
  baby new potatoes
1 bulb of garlic, separated into
  cloves
3 tbsp olive oil
sea salt and freshly ground
  black pepper
1.5 kg / 3 lb 5 oz chicken
a handful of fresh sage leaves

Method

1. Preheat the oven to 200°C (180°C fan) / 400F / gas 6.

2. Boil the potatoes in salted water for 10 minutes then drain well.

3. Mix the potatoes and garlic cloves together in a large roasting tin, then drizzle with olive oil and season with salt and pepper.

4. Season the chicken all over with sea salt and lay it breast-side down on top of the vegetables.

5. Transfer the tin to the oven and roast for 1 hour 10 minutes, turning the chicken over, adding the sage and stirring the vegetables halfway through.

6. To test if the chicken is cooked, insert a skewer into the thickest part of the thigh. If the juices run clear with no trace of blood, it is ready.

Smart tip

Cooking the chicken breast-side down for half of the time keeps the white meat juicy.

Lamb and carrot lattice pie

Preparation time
15 minutes

Cooking time
1 hour 5 minutes

Serves 4

Ingredients

4 tbsp olive oil
1 onion, finely chopped
350 g / 12 ½ oz / 2 ⅓ cups
    lamb shoulder, diced
1 large carrot, chopped
3 cloves of garlic, finely
    chopped
75 g / 2 ½ oz / ⅓ cup dried
    apricots, chopped
100 ml / 3 ½ fl. oz / ½ cup
    dry white wine
100 ml / 3 ½ fl. oz / ½ cup
    lamb or vegetable stock
salt and freshly ground
    black pepper
250 g / 9 oz / ¾ cup all-butter
    puff pastry
1 egg, beaten

Method

1. Heat the oil in a pan and fry the onion and lamb together for 5 minutes. Add the carrot and garlic and cook for a further 5 minutes, then stir in the apricots.

2. Pour in the wine and stock, then simmer very gently with the lid on for 30 minutes. Season to taste with salt and pepper, then tip into a pie dish and leave to cool.

3. Preheat the oven to 220°C (200°C fan) / 425F / gas 7.

4. Roll out the pastry on a floured surface and cut it into strips. Arrange the pastry strips in a lattice formation on top of the lamb, then trim the edges and press down onto the dish to seal.

5. Brush the pastry with egg, then bake for 25 minutes or until the pastry is cooked and golden brown on top.

Beef and Red Leicester bagel

Preparation time
5 minutes

Cooking time
2 minutes

Serves 4

Ingredients

4 poppy seed bagels
1 tbsp Dijon mustard
4 slices rare roast beef
4 slices tomato
4 slices Red Leicester cheese
2 iceberg lettuce leaves,
  shredded

Method

1. Split the bagels in half horizontally and spread thinly with mustard.

2. Top each base with a slice of beef, a slice of tomato and a piece of cheese, then lightly melt the cheese using a blow torch or preheated grill.

3. Top with shredded iceberg and put the tops on, then serve immediately.

Smart tip

Lightly melting the cheese gives these sandwiches a great texture and taste.

Smart tip

Lining the roasting tin with greaseproof paper makes it easier to wash up afterwards.

Roast pork with parsnips and pears

Preparation time
10 minutes

Cooking time
1 hour 40 minutes

Serves 6

Ingredients

1.5 kg / 3 lb 5 oz pork loin
joint, skinned, boned
and rolled
4 tbsp olive oil
2 tbsp fresh thyme leaves
salt and freshly ground
black pepper
6 small parsnips, peeled and
halved lengthways
3 firm pears, peeled, cored
and quartered
6 cloves of garlic, unpeeled
200 ml / 7 fl. oz / ¾ cup
Marsala

Method

1. Preheat the oven to 180°C (160°C fan) / 350F / gas 4.

2. Transfer the pork to a roasting tin lined with greaseproof paper and brush with half of the oil. Sprinkle with thyme and season well with salt and pepper.

3. Roast the pork for 45 minutes.

4. Rub the parsnips, pears and garlic with the rest of the oil and arrange around the pork, then season with salt and pepper.

5. Pour over the Marsala then transfer the tin to the oven and roast for a further 55 minutes, turning the vegetables halfway through.

6. Cover the roasting tin with a double layer of foil and leave to rest for 10 minutes before carving and serving.

Stuffed round courgettes

Preparation time
20 minutes

Cooking time
50 minutes

Serves 6

Ingredients

2 tbsp olive oil
1 onion, finely chopped
1 fennel bulb, finely chopped
½ tsp fennel seeds, crushed
2 cloves of garlic, crushed
250 g / 9 oz / 1 cup minced
   chicken or turkey
250 g / 9 oz / 1 cup pork
   sausage meat
50 g / 1 ¾ oz / ⅔ cup fresh
   white breadcrumbs
4 tbsp Parmesan, finely grated
1 egg yolk
salt and freshly ground
   black pepper
6 round courgettes (zucchinis)

Method

1. Preheat the oven to 190°C (170°C fan) / 375F / gas 5.

2. Heat the oil in a frying pan and fry the onion, fennel bulb and fennel seeds for 5 minutes or until softened. Add the garlic and cook for 2 more minutes, stirring constantly, then transfer to a large mixing bowl.

3. Add the mince, sausage meat, breadcrumbs, Parmesan and egg yolk and mix everything together to form a stuffing, then season with salt and pepper.

4. Cut off the courgette tops and reserve. Hollow out and discard the insides, then pack the cavities with the stuffing mixture.

5. Put the tops back on the courgettes and bake for 40 minutes or until the stuffing is cooked through to the centre and the courgettes are tender to the point of a knife.

Smart tip

Use a teaspoon or
melon baller to hollow
out the courgettes.

Smart tip

Baking the pastry cases blind will ensure the pastry is crisp.

Individual smoked salmon quiches

Preparation time
1 hour

Cooking time
30 minutes

Serves 6

Ingredients

2 tbsp butter
1 large leek, trimmed
    and sliced
3 large eggs
225 ml / 8 fl. oz / ¾ cup
    double (heavy) cream
salt and freshly ground black
    pepper
100 g / 3 ½ oz / ⅔ cup smoked
    salmon, sliced
50 g / 1 ¾ oz / ½ cup soft fresh
    goats' cheese, crumbled
2 tbsp chives, chopped

For the pastry:
100 g / 3 ½ oz / ½ cup butter,
    cubed
200 g / 7 oz / 1 ⅓ cups plain
    (all-purpose) flour

Method

1. To make the pastry, rub the butter into the flour until the mixture resembles fine breadcrumbs. Stir in enough cold water to bring the pastry together into a pliable dough and chill for 30 minutes.

2. Preheat the oven to 190°C (170°C fan) / 375F / gas 5.

3. Roll out the pastry on a floured surface and use it to line six individual tart cases. Prick the pastry with a fork, line with greaseproof baking paper and fill with baking beans or rice. Bake the cases for 10 minutes, then remove the paper and baking beans.

4. Meanwhile, heat the butter in a frying pan and fry the leek for 5 minutes or until softened.

5. Gently whisk the eggs with the cream until smoothly combined, then stir in the leeks and season generously with salt and pepper. Pour the filling into the pastry cases and top with the smoked salmon and goats' cheese.

6. Lower the oven temperature to 150°C (130°C fan) / 300F / gas 2 and bake for 20 minutes or until just set in the centre. Serve hot or cold, garnished with chives.

Maple-roasted turkey breast with bread sauce

Preparation time
10 minutes

Cooking time
45 minutes

Serves 4

Ingredients

900 g / 2 lb turkey breast
3 tbsp butter, melted
3 tbsp maple syrup
1 tsp Dijon mustard
1 tsp ground mixed spice
flat leaf parsley to garnish

For the bread sauce:
600 ml / 1 pint / 2 ½ cups
    whole (full-fat) milk
1 onion, halved
4 cloves
8 black peppercorns
2 bay leaves
100 g / 3 ½ oz / 1 ⅓ cups fresh
    white breadcrumbs
salt and freshly ground black
    pepper
¼ tsp ground nutmeg
¼ tsp ground cinnamon

Method

1. Preheat the oven to 190°C (170°C fan) / 375F / gas 5.

2. Lay the turkey breast in a roasting tin. Mix together the butter, maple syrup, mustard and mixed spice and brush it over the top.

3. Roast the turkey for 45 minutes or until the juices run clear when pierced with a skewer.

4. Meanwhile, pour the milk into a small saucepan and add the onion, cloves, peppercorns and bay leaves.

5. Bring to a very gentle simmer, then turn the heat down to its lowest setting and infuse for 15 minutes.

6. Pass the mixture through a sieve to remove the aromatics and return the milk to the pan. Stir in the breadcrumbs, then cook over a low heat for 3–4 minutes or until the sauce has thickened.

7. Season to taste with salt and pepper, then spoon the sauce into a bowl and sprinkle with the spices. Carve the turkey breast into slices, garnish with parsley and serve with the sauce on the side.

Smart tip

If the turkey starts to brown too quickly, cover the tin with foil.

Smart tip

Finishing the steaks in the oven makes sure they're warm all the way through whilst still being cooked medium.

Fillet steak with Cambozola

Preparation time
15 minutes

Cooking time
7 minutes

Serves 2

Ingredients

2 x 225 g / 8 oz fillet steaks
sea salt and freshly ground
    black pepper
1 tbsp butter
2 slices Cambozola cheese

For the salad:
75 g / 2 ½ oz / ⅓ cup red
    seedless grapes, halved
75 g / 2 ½ oz / ⅓ cup green
    seedless grapes, halved
a handful of lamb's lettuce
2 tbsp hazelnuts (cobnuts),
    roughly chopped
2 tbsp hazelnut (cobnut) oil
salt and freshly ground
    black pepper

Method

1. Preheat the oven to 200°C (180°C fan) / 400F / gas 6 and put a frying pan on to heat for 5 minutes or until smoking hot.

2. Dry the steaks really well with kitchen paper, then season liberally with sea salt and black pepper.

3. Transfer the steaks to the frying pan and cook without disturbing for 3 minutes. Turn them over, add the butter and transfer the pan to the oven for 4 minutes.

4. Baste the steaks with butter from the pan, then transfer to a warm plate, top with the cheese and leave to rest for 5 minutes.

5. Toss the grapes with the lamb's lettuce and hazelnuts and dress with the oil and a little salt and pepper. Serve with the steaks.

Fettuccini with walnut meatballs

Preparation time
50 minutes

Cooking time
55 minutes

Serves 6

Ingredients

2 tbsp olive oil
1 onion, finely chopped
2 cloves of garlic, crushed
400 g / 14 oz / 1 ¾ cups
    canned cherry tomatoes
600 g / 1 lb 4 oz / 5 ½ cups
    dried fettuccini
2 tbsp basil leaves, shredded

For the meatballs:
4 tbsp olive oil
1 onion, finely chopped
1 clove of garlic, crushed
250 g / 9 oz / 1 ⅔ cups
    coarsely minced pork
250 g / 9 oz / 1 ⅔ cups
    sausage meat
50 g / 1 ¾ oz / ⅔ cup fresh
    white breadcrumbs
4 tbsp walnuts, finely chopped
2 tbsp flat leaf parsley,
    finely chopped
2 tbsp basil leaves,
    finely chopped
1 egg yolk

Method

1. To make the meatballs, heat half of the oil in a large sauté pan and fry the onion for 5 minutes or until softened. Add the garlic and cook for 2 more minutes, stirring constantly, then scrape the mixture into a mixing bowl and leave to cool.

2. Add the mince, sausage meat, breadcrumbs, walnuts, herbs and egg yolk and mix well, then shape into golf-ball-sized meatballs. Chill the meatballs for 30 minutes.

3. Heat the rest of the oil in the sauté pan and sear the meatballs on all sides.

4. To make the sauce, heat the oil in a saucepan and gently fry the onion for 10 minutes to soften. Stir in the garlic and cook for 1 minute, then stir in the tomatoes and simmer for 5 minutes.

5. Tip the sauce into the meatball pan and return to a simmer. Cook gently for 30 minutes or until the meatballs are cooked through and the sauce has reduced a little.

6. Boil the pasta in salted water according to the packet instructions or until al dente. Drain the pasta and divide between six warm bowls, then spoon over the meatballs and sauce and sprinkle with shredded basil.

Smart tip

Chilling the meatballs before cooking will stop them from crumbling in the pan.

Smart tip

Use a tart eating apple such as a Braeburn for a nice sharp contrast with the sweet honey.

Lamb chops with apple and broccoli

Preparation time
10 minutes

Cooking time
25 minutes

Serves 4

Ingredients

2 tbsp runny honey
1 tbsp Dijon mustard
2 tbsp olive oil
8 lamb chops
1 head of broccoli,
    cut into florets
2 eating apples, cored
    and cut into wedges
fresh sage leaves to garnish

Method

1. Preheat the oven to 200°C (180°C fan) / 400F / gas 6.

2. Stir together the honey, mustard and oil, then massage the mixture into the lamb, broccoli and apple slices.

3. Season well with salt and pepper then spread out in a roasting tin. Roast for 25 minutes or until the lamb is cooked to your liking and the broccoli is tender.

4. Garnish with sage leaves and serve immediately.

Meatloaf with roasted carrots

Preparation time
25 minutes

Cooking time
45 minutes

Serves 6

Ingredients

2 tbsp olive oil
1 onion, finely chopped
1 carrot, grated
1 parsnip, grated
2 cloves of garlic, crushed
250 g / 9 oz / 1 cup minced
   turkey
250 g / 9 oz / 1 cup pork
   sausage meat
50 g / 1 ¾ oz / ⅔ cup fresh
   white breadcrumbs
3 tbsp flat leaf parsley, finely
   chopped
1 egg yolk
salt and freshly ground
   black pepper

For the carrots:
450 g / 1 lb / 2 ⅔ cups baby
   carrots, scrubbed
3 tbsp olive oil
1 tbsp fresh rosemary,
   chopped
½ tbsp fresh thyme leaves
1 tbsp flat leaf parsley,
   chopped

Method

1. Preheat the oven to 190°C (170°C fan) / 375F / gas 5.

2. Heat the oil in a frying pan and fry the onion, carrot and parsnip for 10 minutes or until softened.

3. Add the garlic and cook for 2 more minutes, stirring constantly, then transfer to a large mixing bowl.

4. Add the mince, sausage meat, breadcrumbs, parsley and egg yolk and mix all together.

5. Season with salt and pepper then shape the mixture into a loaf and transfer to a roasting tin.

6. Transfer the dish to the oven and bake for 45 minutes or until cooked through and golden brown.

7. Once the meatloaf is in the oven, arrange the carrots in a second roasting tin, drizzle with oil and sprinkle with rosemary, salt and pepper. Roast the carrots for 35 minutes, then garnish with thyme and parsley.

8. Cut the meatloaf into slices and serve with the carrots.

Smart tip

Adding grated vegetables to the meatloaf makes the meat go further and adds nutrients.

Smart tip

You can assemble the moussaka in advance and store it in the fridge before baking, but increase the cooking time to 50 minutes.

Vegetable moussaka

Preparation time
1 hour

Cooking time
35 minutes

Serves 6

Ingredients

3 tbsp olive oil
1 onion, finely chopped
3 cloves of garlic, crushed
½ cauliflower, cubed
1 orange pepper, sliced
400 g / 14 oz / 2 cups canned
    tomatoes, chopped
1 vegetable stock cube

For the aubergine layer:
3 aubergines (eggplants), cut
    into 1 cm (½ in) slices
4 tbsp olive oil
salt and freshly ground
    black pepper

For the topping:
2 tbsp butter
1 ½ tbsp plain (all-purpose) flour
¼ tsp dried oregano
300 ml / 10 ½ fl. oz / 1 ¼ cups
    whole milk
75 g / 2 ½ oz / ¾ cup feta
    cheese, crumbled
4 tbsp Parmesan, finely grated
coriander (cilantro) leaves to
    garnish

Method

1. Preheat the oven to 200°C (180°C fan) / 400F / gas 6.

2. Heat the oil in a sauté pan and fry the onion for 10 minutes or until softened. Add the garlic and cook for 2 more minutes. Add the cauliflower and orange pepper and stir-fry for 5 minutes.

3. Add the chopped tomatoes and stock cube and bring to a simmer, then cook over a low heat for 30 minutes.

4. Meanwhile, brush the aubergine slices with oil and season with salt and pepper, then cook in batches on a smoking hot griddle for 2 minutes on each side or until nicely marked.

5. Melt the butter in a small saucepan. Stir in the flour and oregano then gradually incorporate the milk, stirring continuously to avoid any lumps forming. Simmer the sauce until it thickens, then stir in the feta and season to taste with salt and pepper.

6. Line a baking dish with half of the griddled aubergine slices and top with the vegetable sauce. Arrange the rest of the aubergine slices on top, then pour over the feta sauce and sprinkle with Parmesan.

7. Bake the moussaka for 35 minutes or until cooked through and golden brown on top. Garnish with coriander leaves before serving.

Chicken and kale cannelloni

Preparation time
45 minutes

Cooking time
20 minutes

Serves 4

Ingredients

4 tbsp butter
2 shallots, chopped
2 cloves of garlic, crushed
3 skinless chicken breasts,
   diced
200 g / 7 oz / 3 cups curly kale,
   chopped
2 tbsp plain (all-purpose) flour
600 ml / 1 pint / 2 ½ cups milk
200 g / 7 oz / 2 cups Gruyère,
   grated
freshly ground black pepper
16 sheets ready-made
   fresh pasta

Method

1. Preheat the oven to 200°C (180°C fan) / 400F / gas 6.

2. Melt half the butter in a frying pan and fry the shallots
    and garlic for 5 minutes. Add the chicken and stir-fry for
    3 minutes, then stir in the kale and cover with a lid.
    Steam for 4 minutes, then stir well.

3. Meanwhile, melt the rest of the butter in a small saucepan.
    Stir in the flour then gradually incorporate the milk, stirring
    continuously to avoid any lumps forming.

4. When the mixture starts to bubble, stir in half the cheese and
    a grind of black pepper, then take the pan off the heat.

5. Add a third of the sauce to the chicken mixture and stir.

6. Split the chicken filling between the pasta sheets, then roll
    them up and pack them into four individual gratin dishes.

7. Pour over the rest of the sauce and sprinkle with the
    other half of the cheese, then bake for 20 minutes or until
    golden brown.

Smart tip

Adding some of the sauce to the chicken mixture binds it together and makes the cannelloni easier to roll.

Smart tip

Make a big batch of mushy peas in advance and freeze, then just reheat a portion when needed.

Fish, chips and mushy peas

Preparation time
1 hour 30 minutes

Cooking time
50 minutes

Serves 4

Ingredients

200 g / 7 oz / 1 ⅓ cups plain
  (all-purpose) flour
2 tbsp olive oil
250 ml / 9 fl. oz / 1 cup
  pale ale
4 portions white fish fillet

For the chips:
4 large Maris Piper potatoes,
  peeled and cut into chips
sunflower oil for deep-frying

For the peas:
150 g / 5 ½ oz / 1 cup dried
  marrowfat peas, soaked
  overnight
1 tsp caster (superfine) sugar
salt and freshly ground black
  pepper

Method

1. Soak the chips in cold water for 1 hour to reduce the starch. Drain the chips and dry completely with a clean tea towel, then air-dry on a wire rack for 30 minutes.

2. Meanwhile, drain the peas of their soaking water and put them in a small saucepan with the sugar, a pinch of salt and pepper and enough cold water to cover. Simmer for 25 minutes or until the water has evaporated and the peas have turned to mush.

3. To make the batter for the fish, sieve the flour into a bowl then whisk in the olive oil and ale until smoothly combined.

4. Heat the sunflower oil in a deep fat fryer, according to the manufacturer's instructions, to a temperature of 130°C (265F).

5. Par-cook the chips for 10 minutes so that they cook all the way through but don't brown. Drain the chips on plenty of kitchen paper to absorb the excess oil.

6. Increase the fryer temperature to 180°C (350F). Dip the fish in the batter and fry for 4 minutes or until golden brown. Transfer the fish to a bowl lined with kitchen paper and increase the fryer temperature to 190°C (375F).

7. Return the chips to the fryer basket and cook for 4–5 minutes or until crisp and golden brown. Drain the chips of excess oil and serve with the fish and mushy peas.

Braised lamb shanks with carrots

Preparation time
20 minutes

Cooking time
2 hours

Serves 4

Ingredients

2 tbsp olive oil
4 lamb shanks
1 onion, quartered and sliced
3 thick rashers streaky bacon, sliced
2 cloves of garlic, finely chopped
4 carrots, peeled and cut into batons
100 ml / 3 ½ fl. oz / ½ cup dry white wine
400 ml / 14 fl. oz / 1 ⅔ cups vegetable stock
salt and freshly ground black pepper
a small bunch of young rosemary tips

Method

1. Preheat the oven to 180°C (160°C fan) / 350F / gas 4.
2. Heat the oil in a large frying pan and sear the lamb shanks all over. Transfer to a plate and add the onion and bacon to the pan. Fry for 5 minutes or until lightly browned, then add the garlic and cook for 1 more minute.
3. Scrape the onion mixture into a large roasting tin or baking dish and mix with the carrots, wine and stock. Nestle the lamb shanks in the dish and season well with salt and pepper.
4. Wrap the dish in a double layer of foil, sealing the edges tightly, then transfer it to the oven and bake for 2 hours or until the lamb is very tender.
5. Remove the foil and garnish with rosemary before serving.

Smart tip

Searing the lamb first helps to enhance the taste of the meat.

Smart tip

Ask the fishmonger to prepare the fish by cutting off the head and tail and boning it from the inside before removing the skin.

Salmon en croûte

Preparation time
45 minutes

Cooking time
35 minutes

Serves 8

Ingredients

450 g / 1 lb / 1 ½ cups
  all-butter puff pastry
1 small salmon, skinned,
  butterflied and boned
1 egg, beaten

For the filling:

1 carrot, peeled and diced
50 g / 1 ¾ oz / ½ cup green
  beans, chopped
1 lemon, zest finely grated
200 g / 7 oz / 1 cup fresh
  ricotta
2 large egg yolks

Method

1. Preheat the oven to 230°C (210°C fan) / 450F / gas 8.

2. To make the filling, cook the carrot and beans in salted, boiling water for 6 minutes, then drain well and plunge into cold water. Drain again, then dry with kitchen paper.

3. Beat the lemon zest, ricotta and egg yolks together, then stir in the vegetables.

4. On a floured surface, roll out the pastry into a large rectangle. Open out the salmon on top of the pastry and spoon the filling in a line down the centre.

5. Close the salmon, then bring up the pastry sides and crimp tightly to seal. Turn the parcel over so that the join is underneath and seal the ends in the same way. Trim away any excess pastry, then use a paring knife to mark on the scales and brush with beaten egg.

6. Bake for 35 minutes or until the pastry is golden and cooked through underneath.

Shepherd's pie with leeks

Preparation time
15 minutes

Cooking time
50 minutes

Serves 4

Ingredients

2 tbsp butter
3 leeks, trimmed and chopped
2 cloves of garlic, finely
  chopped
450 g / 1 lb / 3 cups lamb
  mince
150 ml / 5 ½ fl. oz / ⅔ cup lamb
  stock
150 ml / 5 ½ fl. oz / ⅔ cup
  double (heavy) cream
¼ tsp freshly grated nutmeg

For the topping:
450 g / 1 lb / 3 cups floury
  potatoes, peeled and
  cubed
100 ml / 3 ½ fl. oz / ½ cup milk
50 g / 1 ¾ oz / ¼ cup butter
25 g / 1 oz / ⅓ cup fine
  breadcrumbs

Method

1. Heat the butter in a sauté pan and fry the leeks and garlic over a low heat for 10 minutes to soften. Turn up the heat, add the lamb mince and stir-fry for 5 minutes or until lightly browned.

2. Add the stock and cream to the pan, then reduce the heat and simmer for 20 minutes or until the sauce is thick.

3. Meanwhile, boil the potatoes in salted water for 12 minutes, or until they are tender, then drain well. Return the potatoes to the saucepan and add the milk and butter, then mash until smooth.

4. Preheat the oven to 200°C (180°C fan) / 400F / gas 6.

5. Stir the nutmeg into the lamb, then season to taste with salt and pepper. Spoon the lamb into a gratin dish and top with the mashed potato. Sprinkle with breadcrumbs and bake for 15 minutes or until the top is golden brown.

Smart tip

Cooking the leeks long and slow gives them the sweetest taste.

Smart tip

Attach the pastry decorations with a dab of beaten egg.

Individual curried chicken pies

Preparation time
30 minutes

Cooking time
30 minutes

Makes 4

Ingredients

2 tbsp butter
1 onion, finely chopped
50 g / 1 ¾ oz / ½ cup green
  beans, cut into short lengths
2 cloves of garlic, crushed
½ tbsp fresh root ginger,
  finely chopped
2 tsp mild curry powder
1 tsp plain (all-purpose) flour
250 ml / 9 fl. oz / 1 cup
  coconut milk
200 g / 7 oz / 1 cup cooked
  chicken breast, sliced
1 tbsp coriander (cilantro)
  leaves, finely chopped
salt and white pepper
800 g / 1 lb 12 oz / 2 ¾ cups
  all-butter puff pastry
1 egg, beaten

Method

1. Preheat the oven to 200°C (180°C fan) / 400F / gas 6.

2. Heat the butter in a saucepan and gently fry the onion and beans for 5 minutes. Add the garlic and ginger and cook for 2 more minutes.

3. Sprinkle in the curry powder and flour and stir well, then stir in the coconut milk and bubble until it thickens slightly.

4. Add the chicken and coriander to the pan and heat through, then season to taste with salt and white pepper.

5. Roll out half the pastry on a lightly floured surface and use it to line four individual pie dishes. Divide the filling between the pastry cases and brush the rims with water.

6. Roll out the rest of the pastry and top each pie with a pastry lid. Press round the edges to seal, then cut away any excess pastry and use the trimmings to decorate the tops.

7. Brush the pies with beaten egg and bake for 30 minutes or until the pastry is cooked through underneath and golden brown on top.

Lasagne

Preparation time
15 minutes

Cooking time
1 hour 30 minutes

Serves 6

Ingredients

4 tbsp olive oil
1 onion, finely chopped
1 carrot, finely chopped
1 celery stick, finely chopped
3 cloves of garlic, crushed
450 g / 1 lb / 2 cups minced
   beef
400 g / 14 oz / 2 cups canned
   tomatoes, chopped
1 beef stock cube
2 tbsp butter
2 tbsp plain (all-purpose) flour
600 ml / 1 pint / 2 ½ cups
   whole milk
salt and freshly ground
   black pepper
400 g / 14 oz dried
   lasagne sheets
4 tbsp Parmesan, finely grated

Method

1. Preheat the oven to 200°C (180°C fan) / 400F / gas 6 and
    butter a large baking dish. Heat the oil in a sauté pan and fry
    the onion, carrot and celery for 10 minutes or until softened.
    Add the garlic and cook for 2 more minutes. Add the mince
    and stir-fry until browned.

2. Add the chopped tomatoes and stock cube and bring to a
    simmer, then cook over a low heat for 30 minutes.

3. Meanwhile, melt the butter in a small saucepan. Stir in
    the flour, then gradually incorporate the milk, stirring
    continuously to avoid any lumps forming. Simmer the sauce
    until it thickens, then season to taste with salt and pepper.

4. Starting with a layer of lasagne sheets, layer up the meat
    sauce, white sauce and pasta until everything has been
    used, finishing with a layer of white sauce.

5. Sprinkle the top with Parmesan, then bake the lasagne for
    45 minutes or until the top is golden brown and the pasta is
    tender all the way through.

Smart tip

Buttering the
baking dish stops
the base layer of
pasta from sticking.

Smart tip

Don't over mix the mashed potato or the starches will turn gluey.

Ham and leek potato-topped pie

Preparation time
40 minutes

Cooking time
30 minutes

Serves 6

Ingredients

450 g / 1 lb / 3 cups potatoes,
  peeled and cubed
4 tbsp butter
2 tbsp plain (all-purpose) flour
500 ml / 17 ½ fl. oz / 2 cups
  milk
3 tbsp olive oil
3 leeks, chopped
200 g / 7 oz / 1 ⅓ cups cooked
  ham, sliced
salt and freshly ground
  black pepper
75 g / 2 ½ oz / ¾ cup Cheddar,
  grated
1 tbsp flat leaf parsley,
  chopped

Method

1. Preheat the oven to 200°C (180°C fan) / 400F / gas 6.

2. Cook the potatoes in boiling, salted water for 12 minutes or
    until tender then drain well.

3. Heat half of the butter in a small saucepan and stir in the
    flour. Reserve 100 ml / 3 ½ fl. oz / ½ cup of the milk for the
    potatoes and slowly incorporate the rest into the butter and
    flour mixture, stirring constantly. Cook until the sauce is thick
    and smooth.

4. Heat the oil in a frying pan and fry the leeks for 10 minutes
    or until soft, then stir them into the sauce with the ham.
    Season to taste with salt and pepper, then scrape the
    mixture into a baking dish.

5. Mash the potatoes with the reserved milk and remaining
    butter and spoon on top of the leek and ham mixture.

6. Sprinkle with cheese and parsley, then bake for 30 minutes
    or until the topping is golden brown.

Ham and pea pasta bake

Preparation time
20 minutes

Cooking time
45 minutes

Serves 4

Ingredients

400 g / 14 oz / 2 ¾ cups dried
  casarecce pasta
2 tbsp butter
2 tbsp plain (all-purpose) flour
600 ml / 1 pint / 2 ½ cups milk
100 g / 3 ½ oz / 1 cup
  mangetout
150 g / 5 ½ oz / 1 cup peas,
  defrosted if frozen
6 slices prosciutto, chopped
75 g / 2 ½ oz / ¾ cup
  Parmesan, finely grated
salt and freshly ground
  black pepper
4 tbsp breadcrumbs

Method

1. Preheat the oven to 180°C (160°C fan) / 350F / gas 4.
2. Cook the pasta in boiling, salted water for 10 minutes or until almost cooked. Drain well.
3. Meanwhile, melt the butter in a medium saucepan and stir in the flour.
4. Gradually whisk in the milk a little at a time until it is all incorporated.
5. Cook the sauce over a low heat, stirring constantly, until the mixture thickens. Beat vigorously to remove any lumps.
6. Take the pan off the heat and stir in the mangetout, peas, prosciutto and 3 tbsp of Parmesan. Season to taste with salt and pepper.
7. Stir the pasta into the sauce and scrape it into a baking dish.
8. Mix the rest of the Parmesan with the breadcrumbs and sprinkle it over the top, then bake for 45 minutes or until the top is golden brown and the pasta is cooked.

Smart tip

You may not need very much salt for the sauce as the prosciutto is quite salty.

Smart tip

Rest the dough in a warm, draught-free place for the best rise.

Ham and mushroom pizza

Preparation time
1 hour 45 minutes

Cooking time
15 minutes

Makes 1

Ingredients

200 g / 7 oz / 1 ⅓ cups strong white bread flour, plus extra for dusting
½ tsp easy-blend yeast
1 tsp caster (superfine) sugar
½ tsp fine sea salt
1 tbsp olive oil
3 tbsp tomato pizza sauce
3 slices cooked ham, chopped
4 button mushrooms, sliced
1 mozzarella ball, sliced
½ tsp dried oregano

Method

1. Mix together the flour, yeast, sugar and salt and stir the oil into 140 ml / 4 ½ fl. oz / ⅔ cup of warm water. Stir the liquid into the dry ingredients, then knead on a lightly oiled surface for 10 minutes or until smooth and elastic.

2. Leave the dough to rest covered with oiled cling film for 1 hour or until doubled in size.

3. Preheat the oven to 220°C (200°C fan) / 425F / gas 7 and grease a non-stick baking tray.

4. Knead the dough for 2 more minutes, then roll out thinly into a circle and transfer to the baking tray. Spread the dough with the pizza sauce and top with the ham, mushrooms and mozzarella.

5. Sprinkle with oregano and bake for 15 minutes or until the pizza dough is cooked through underneath and the cheese is bubbling.

Pot-roasted beef with chicory

Preparation time
10 minutes

Cooking time
1 hour 45 minutes

Serves 8

Ingredients

3 kg / 6 lb 10 oz topside
of beef
salt and freshly ground
black pepper
2 tbsp beef dripping
500 ml / 17 fl. oz / 2 cups dry
white wine
4 heads of chicory (endive),
quartered
4 cloves of garlic, sliced

Method

1. Preheat the oven to 180°C (160°C fan) / 350F / gas 4 and season the beef well with salt and pepper.
2. Heat the beef dripping in a large roasting tin, then sear the beef until well browned all over.
3. Pour in the wine and let it simmer for 2 minutes, then add the chicory and garlic to the pan and cover it tightly with a double layer of foil.
4. Transfer the tin to the oven and roast for 1 hour 30 minutes.
5. Remove the foil 30 minutes before the end of the cooking time to brown the beef and chicory.

Smart tip

Pot-roasting part-steams and part-roasts the meat, making it tender and juicy.

Stews and Casseroles

Lamb, pepper and fig tagine

Preparation time
3 hours 15 minutes

Cooking time
2 hours

Serves 6

Ingredients

2 tsp ras el hanout spice mix
2 tbsp runny honey
2 tbsp olive oil
800 g / 1 lb 12 oz / 5 ⅓ cups
    lamb shoulder, cut into
    large chunks
1 onion, quartered and sliced
3 cloves of garlic, finely
    chopped
150 g / 5 ½ oz / ¾ cup dried
    figs, halved
2 orange peppers, halved
    and sliced
1 bay leaf
1 tbsp fresh thyme leaves
500 ml / 17 ½ fl. oz / 2 cups
    good quality lamb stock
salt and freshly ground
    black pepper

Method

1. Stir the ras el hanout, honey and oil together, then massage
   it into the lamb and leave to marinate for at least 3 hours.

2. Preheat the oven to 160°C (140°C fan) / 325F / gas 3.

3. Stir the rest of the ingredients into the lamb in a tagine or
   cast iron casserole dish and season well with salt
   and pepper.

4. Cover the dish and cook in the oven for 2 hours, or until the
   lamb is tender.

Smart tip

Marinating the lamb
before cooking gives a
delicious taste to
the dish.

Smart tip

The broad beans and potatoes give the sauce a lovely thick texture.

Beef, vegetable and bean casserole

Preparation time
20 minutes

Cooking time
3 hours

Serves 6

Ingredients

900 g / 2 lb / 5 cups beef shin, boned and cut into chunks
salt and freshly ground black pepper
2 tbsp olive oil
1 onion, chopped
2 large carrots, cut into chunks
2 bay leaves
800 ml / 1 pint 8 fl. oz / 3 ¼ cups beef stock
100 g / 3 ½ oz / ⅔ cup dried broad beans (fava beans), soaked overnight
450 g / 1 lb / 3 cups potatoes, peeled and cut into large chunks
curly parsley to garnish

Method

1. Preheat the oven to 160°C (140°C fan) / 325F / gas 3 and season the beef liberally with salt and pepper.

2. Heat the oil in a large cast iron casserole dish over a high heat, then sear the beef until browned all over.

3. Remove the meat from the pan, lower the heat and add the onions. Cook for 5 minutes, stirring occasionally until softened. Add the carrots and bay leaves and cook for 2 more minutes.

4. Increase the heat, then pour in the stock and bring to a simmer. Return the beef to the pot and add the broad beans, then cover the dish and transfer it to the oven to cook for 2 hours.

5. Give the pot a good stir and add the potatoes, then cover the dish and return it to the oven for a further hour. Season to taste and serve garnished with parsley.

Smoked fish casserole

Preparation time
15 minutes

Cooking time
1 hour 30 minutes

Serves 6

Ingredients

2 tbsp olive oil
1 onion, chopped
100 g / 3 ½ oz / ½ cup smoked lardons
1 fennel bulb, julienned
1 large carrot, julienned
450 g / 1 lb / 3 cups waxy potatoes, peeled and cut into large chunks
3 bay leaves
a few sprigs of thyme
800 ml / 1 pint 8 oz / 3 ¼ cups vegetable stock
175 g / 6 oz / 1 ½ cups small Brussels sprouts
1 smoked haddock fillet, skinned and cut into chunks
3 smoked mackerel fillets, skinned and flaked
salt and freshly ground black pepper

Method

1. Preheat the oven to 160°C (140°C fan) / 325F / gas 3.

2. Heat the oil in a large cast iron casserole dish and fry the onion, lardons and fennel for 10 minutes. Add the carrots, potatoes and herbs, then pour in the stock.

3. Increase the heat and bring to a simmer, then cover the dish and transfer it to the oven to cook for 1 hour.

4. Give the pot a good stir and add the sprouts and haddock, then cover the dish and return it to the oven for 30 minutes.

5. Stir in the mackerel, then season to taste with salt and pepper and serve.

Smart tip

As the mackerel is hot-smoked, it only needs to be warmed through.

Smart tip

Sear the veal in batches so you don't overcrowd the pan.

Creamy veal and wild mushroom casserole

Preparation time
15 minutes

Cooking time
2 hours 10 minutes

Serves 4

Ingredients

800 g / 1 lb 12 oz / 4 cups veal shoulder, cubed
salt and freshly ground black pepper
4 tbsp plain (all-purpose) flour
5 tbsp butter
450 g / 1 lb / 2 cups baby onions, peeled
1 celery stick, finely chopped
1 clove of garlic, crushed
600 ml / 1 pint / 2 ½ cups light veal or chicken stock
300 ml / 10 ½ fl. oz / 1 ¼ cups double (heavy) cream
150 g / 5 ½ oz / 2 cups wild mushrooms, chopped if large
2 tbsp chervil, chopped

Method

1. Preheat the oven to 160°C (140°C fan) / 325F / gas 3.

2. Season the veal with salt and pepper then dust the pieces with flour. Heat 3 tbsp of the butter in a large cast iron casserole dish and sear the veal until golden brown, then remove to a plate.

3. Add the onions, celery and garlic to the pan and stir-fry for 3 minutes, then pour in the stock and bring to the boil.

4. Return the veal to the casserole, then cover and transfer to the oven to cook for 2 hours.

5. Stir in the cream and season to taste with salt and pepper, then return to the oven while you cook the mushrooms.

6. Heat the rest of the butter in a frying pan and sauté the mushrooms for 5 minutes or until golden.

7. Stir the mushrooms into the casserole then serve, garnished with chervil.

Scallop and leek stew

Preparation time
5 minutes

Cooking time
12 minutes

Serves 2

Ingredients

2 tbsp butter
1 leek, trimmed and sliced
2 cloves of garlic, crushed
150 ml / 5 ½ fl. oz / ⅔ cup dry
    white wine
150 ml / 5 ½ fl. oz / ⅔ cup
    double (heavy) cream
8 scallops, halved horizontally
½ tbsp French tarragon,
    chopped
½ tbsp flat leaf parsley,
    chopped
salt and freshly ground
    black pepper

Method

1. Heat the butter in a saucepan and gently fry the leeks and garlic for 5 minutes or until softened.

2. Turn up the heat and pour in the wine, then simmer until reduced by half. Pour in the cream and lower the heat.

3. When the cream starts to simmer, stir in the scallops and poach gently for 2 minutes or until they just turn translucent.

4. Stir in the herbs and season to taste with salt and pepper, then serve immediately.

Smart tip
Be careful not to overcook the scallops or they'll toughen.

Smart tip
Rinse the rice
under running water
before using.

Pork, rice and vegetable stew

Preparation time
15 minutes

Cooking time
1 hour

Serves 6

Ingredients

2 tbsp butter
750 g / 1 lb 12 oz / 4 ⅔ cups
    pork shoulder, cubed
1 onion, finely chopped
1 celery stick, finely chopped
2 carrots, cut into chunks
1 tsp dried herbs de Provence
200 g / 7 oz / 1 cup long grain
    rice
1 litre / 1 pint 14 fl. oz / 4 cups
    chicken stock
salt and freshly ground
    black pepper
flat leaf parsley to garnish

Method

1. Heat the butter in a large saucepan and fry the pork until golden. Add the onions, celery and carrots and sweat for 10 minutes, then stir in the herbs and rice.

2. Pour in the chicken stock and bring to a simmer, then partially cover the pan and cook gently for 1 hour.

3. Season to taste with salt and pepper and serve garnished with parsley.

Coq au vin

Preparation time
20 minutes

Cooking time
2 hours 30 minutes

Serves 4

Ingredients

8 small chicken legs
salt and freshly ground black
  pepper
3 tbsp plain (all-purpose) flour
1 tsp mustard powder
3 tbsp olive oil
2 tbsp butter
150 g / 5 ½ oz / 1 cup
  pancetta, cubed
200 g / 7 oz / 1 ⅓ cups baby
  onions, peeled
a few sprigs of thyme
600 ml / 1 pint / 2 ½ cups
  red wine
150 g / 5 ½ oz / 2 cups button
  mushrooms, sliced
flat leaf parsley to garnish

Method

1. Preheat the oven to 160°C (140°C fan) / 325F / gas 3.
   Season the chicken well with salt and pepper, then toss with
   the flour and mustard powder to coat.

2. Heat half of the oil and butter in a cast iron casserole dish
   and sear the chicken pieces on all sides.

3. Remove the chicken from the dish and add the rest of
   the oil and butter, followed by the pancetta, onions and
   thyme. Sauté for 5 minutes, then pour in the wine and bring
   to a simmer.

4. Return the chicken to the pot, then cover and cook in the
   oven for 2 hours.

5. Stir in the mushrooms and return to the oven for 30 minutes,
   then taste and adjust the seasoning with salt and pepper
   and serve garnished with parsley.

Smart tip

When the time is up, the chicken should pull easily away from the bone. If not, return to the oven for 20 minutes and test again.

Smart tip
Make sure the lardons and vegetables begin to brown before adding the stock.

Bacon, leek and potato stew

Preparation time
5 minutes

Cooking time
35 minutes

Serves 4

Ingredients

4 tbsp olive oil
2 leeks, sliced
200 g / 7 oz / 1 cup smoked
    lardons
450 g / 1 lb / 2 ½ cups new
    potatoes, quartered
150 g / 5 ½ oz / 2 cups button
    mushrooms, halved
2 cloves of garlic, crushed
400 ml / 14 fl. oz / 1 ⅔ cups
    vegetable stock
2 tbsp flat leaf parsley,
    chopped
a small bunch of chives, cut
    into short lengths

Method

1. Heat the oil in a large sauté pan and stir-fry the leeks and lardons for 3 minutes.

2. Add the potatoes to the pan and fry, stirring occasionally, for 10 minutes or until golden brown.

3. Add the mushrooms and garlic to the pan and stir-fry for 2 minutes, then pour in the stock.

4. Cover and simmer for 10 minutes, then remove the lid and bubble until the stock has reduced to just a few spoonfuls.

5. Season to taste with salt and pepper and serve garnished with parsley and chives.

Chunky beef chilli

Preparation time
15 minutes

Cooking time
2 hours

Serves 6

Ingredients

2 tbsp olive oil
1 carrot, sliced
1 celery stick, sliced
1 red chilli (chilli),
  finely chopped
2 cloves of garlic, crushed
½ tsp Cayenne pepper
½ tsp ground coriander
  (cilantro)
450 g / 1 lb / 2 cups braising
  steak, cubed
400 g / 14 oz / 1 ⅔ cups beef
  stock
400 g / 14 oz / 1 ¾ cups
  canned kidney
  beans, drained
3 spring onions (scallions),
  sliced
2 medium tomatoes, diced
1 green pepper, julienned
1 firm avocado, peeled,
  stoned and diced
salt and freshly ground
  black pepper

Method

1. Heat the oil in a large saucepan and fry the carrot, celery and chilli for 3 minutes, stirring occasionally.

2. Add the garlic, Cayenne and coriander and cook for 2 minutes, then add the beef.

3. Fry the beef until it starts to brown, then add the stock and bring to a gentle simmer.

4. Cover and simmer gently for 2 hours, stirring occasionally.

5. Stir in the kidney beans, spring onions, tomatoes, pepper and avocado and warm through, then taste for seasoning and add salt and freshly ground black pepper as necessary.

Smart tip
Adding the fresh salad
vegetables at the end
gives the dish extra
texture and freshness.

Smart tip

Adding the spinach right at the end retains the nutrients.

Chicken, potato and flageolet bean stew

Preparation time
20 minutes

Cooking time
1 hour

Serves 6

Ingredients

150 g / 5 ½ oz / 1 cup dried
   flageolet beans, soaked
   overnight
150 g / 5 ½ oz / 1 cup dried
   chickpeas (garbanzo
   beans), soaked overnight
2 tbsp olive oil
1 onion, finely chopped
4 cloves of garlic, chopped
4 chicken breasts, skinned
   and sliced
2 medium potatoes, sliced
2 carrots, chopped
400 ml / 14 fl. oz / 1 ⅔ cups
   chicken stock
400 ml / 14 fl. oz / 1 ⅔ cups
   tomato passata
100 g / 3 ½ oz / 4 cups
   spinach, washed

Method

1. Drain the beans and chickpeas from their soaking water and put them in a large saucepan of cold water. Bring to the boil and cook for 10 minutes, then drain well.

2. Meanwhile, heat the oil in a large saucepan and fry the onion and garlic for 5 minutes. Add the chicken and stir-fry until lightly browned.

3. Stir in the drained beans, potatoes, carrots, stock and passata and bring to the boil. Reduce the heat and simmer for 1 hour or until the beans are tender, but still holding their shape.

4. Season to taste with salt and pepper, then stir in the spinach, cover the pan and leave to wilt for 5 minutes before serving.

Mediterranean vegetable stew

Preparation time
5 minutes

Cooking time
35 minutes

Serves 4

Ingredients

3 tbsp olive oil
1 onion, chopped
1 yellow pepper, deseeded
  and cubed
1 red pepper, deseeded
  and cubed
1 aubergine (eggplant), cubed
3 cloves of garlic, crushed
1 tsp chilli (chili) flakes
a pinch of salt
400 g / 14 oz / 2 cups canned
  tomatoes, chopped
2 tbsp flat leaf parsley,
  chopped

Method

1. Heat the oil in a large sauté pan and fry the onion and peppers over a low heat for 10 minutes or until softened and sweet.

2. Add the aubergine, garlic and chilli flakes and sauté for 2 minutes. Add a big pinch of salt, then cover the pan and cook for 5 more minutes, stirring halfway through.

3. Uncover the pan, add the tomatoes and stir well. Simmer with the pan partially covered for 15 minutes or until the vegetables are tender.

4. Season to taste with salt and pepper then serve, garnished with parsley.

Smart tip

Covering the pan when frying the aubergine releases some of the moisture and stops it from absorbing too much oil and burning.

Smart tip

Flouring the turkey
pieces gives body
to the casserole as
it cooks.

Turkey, parsnip and Irish stout casserole

Preparation time
20 minutes

Cooking time
2 hours

Serves 6

Ingredients

900 g / 2 lb / 6 cups turkey
   meat, cubed
salt and freshly ground
   black pepper
4 tbsp plain (all-purpose) flour
2 tbsp olive oil
1 onion, chopped
4 parsnips, cut into chunks
2 bay leaves
2 star anise
800 ml / 1 pint 8 fl. oz /
   3 ¼ cups Irish stout

Method

1. Preheat the oven to 160°C (140°C fan) / 325F / gas 3.
   Season the turkey with salt and pepper, then dust with flour.

2. Heat the oil in a large cast iron casserole dish over a high
   heat, then sear the turkey in batches until browned all over.

3. Remove the meat from the pan, lower the heat and add
   the onions. Cook for 5 minutes, stirring occasionally until
   softened. Add the parsnips, bay leaves and star anise and
   cook for 2 more minutes.

4. Increase the heat then pour in the Irish stout and bring to a
   simmer. Return the turkey to the pot then cover the dish and
   transfer it to the oven to cook for 2 hours.

5. Taste the casserole and season with salt and pepper
   before serving.

Mini casserole of cod with wild garlic pesto

Preparation time
15 minutes

Cooking time
20 minutes

Serves 4

Ingredients

1 tbsp butter
2 leeks, trimmed and chopped
salt and white pepper
4 portions cod fillet
350 ml / 12 fl. oz / 1 ½ cups
  fish stock
50 g / 1 ¾ oz / 2 cups wild
  garlic leaves

For the pesto:
1 ½ tbsp pine nuts, toasted
50 g / 1 ¾ oz / 2 cups wild
  garlic leaves
25 g / 1 oz / ¼ cup Pecorino,
  finely grated
200 ml / 7 fl. oz / ¾ cup extra
  virgin olive oil

Method

1. Preheat the oven to 160°C (140°C fan) / 325F / gas 3.

2. Heat the butter in a frying pan and gently fry the leeks for 5 minutes or until softened. Season with salt and white pepper, then divide between four mini casserole dishes and top with the cod.

3. Pour the stock into the frying pan and bring to the boil, then pour it over the cod and put on the casserole lids.

4. Transfer the casseroles to the oven and cook for 20 minutes.

5. Meanwhile, pound the pine nuts with a pestle and mortar until broken up but not pasty. Add the wild garlic a handful at a time and pound until well pulped, then stir in the cheese and olive oil.

6. When the cod is ready, stir in the wild garlic, then re-cover the pots and let the leaves wilt for 2 minutes.

7. Top the cod with a big spoonful of pesto and serve immediately.

Smart tip

The cod is ready when it has just turned opaque in the centre and flakes easily.

Smart tip

After the first hour and a half of cooking, remove the lid so that the potatoes can crisp.

Lamb hotpot

Preparation time
25 minutes

Cooking time
2 hours 30 minutes

Serves 6

Ingredients

1 kg / 2 lb 3 ½ oz / 7 cups
  boneless lamb neck, cubed
3 lamb kidneys, trimmed and
  quartered
salt and freshly ground
  black pepper
3 tbsp butter
2 tbsp olive oil
2 medium onions, sliced
2 cloves of garlic, crushed
6 sprigs fresh thyme
1 tbsp plain (all-purpose) flour
800 ml / 1 pint 7 fl. oz /
  3 ¼ cups lamb or chicken
  stock
1 kg / 2 lb 3 ½ oz / 6 ½ cups
  potatoes

Method

1. Preheat the oven to 160°C (140°C fan) / 325F / gas 3.

2. Blot the lamb neck and kidneys with kitchen paper to ensure
    they are completely dry, then season liberally with salt and
    pepper. Melt half the butter with the oil in a frying pan over
    a high heat, then sear the lamb and kidneys in batches until
    browned all over.

3. Remove the meat from the pan, lower the heat a little and
    add the onions. Cook for 5 minutes, stirring occasionally
    until softened. Add the garlic and thyme and cook for
    2 more minutes.

4. Increase the heat and stir in the flour, then incorporate the
    stock and bring to a simmer. Arrange the lamb and kidneys
    in a casserole dish and pour over the onion liquor.

5. Slice the potatoes 3 mm thick with a sharp knife or mandolin
    and arrange them on top of the lamb. Cut the remaining
    butter into small pieces and dot it over the top of the
    potatoes, then cover the dish tightly with foil or a lid.
    Bake for 2 hours 30 minutes, then serve immediately.

Tea Time

Strawberry Swiss roll

Preparation time
25 minutes

Cooking time
12 minutes

Serves 6

Ingredients

100 g / 3 ½ oz / ⅔ cup
   self-raising flour
1 tsp baking powder
100 g / 3 ½ oz / ½ cup caster
   (superfine) sugar
100 g / 3 ½ oz/ ½ cup butter
2 large eggs
1 tsp vanilla extract
225 g / 8 oz / ⅔ cup strawberry
   jam (jelly)
icing (confectioners') sugar for
   dusting

Method

1. Preheat the oven to 180°C (160°C fan) / 350F / gas 4 and grease and line a Swiss roll tin with greaseproof paper.

2. Put the flour, baking powder, sugar, butter, eggs and vanilla extract in a large mixing bowl and whisk together with an electric whisk for 4 minutes or until pale and well whipped.

3. Spoon the mixture into the tin and spread into an even layer with a palette knife.

4. Bake for 12 minutes or until the cake is springy to the touch.

5. When the cake is ready, turn it out onto a sheet of greaseproof paper and peel off the lining paper.

6. Spread the cake with the jam, then roll it up tightly and leave to cool.

7. Cut the cake into slices and serve dusted with icing sugar.

Smart tip
Rolling up the cake
whilst warm will prevent
it from cracking.

Smart tip

Keep an eye on the condensed milk as it cooks and top up the pan with water if needed so it doesn't boil dry.

Millionaire's shortbread

Preparation time
20 minutes

Cooking time
3 hours 20 minutes

Serves 12

Ingredients

225 g / 8 oz / 1 ½ cups plain
(all-purpose) flour
75 g / 2 ½ oz / ⅓ cup caster
(superfine) sugar
150 g / 5 oz / ⅔ cup butter,
cubed

For the topping:
400 g / 14 oz canned
condensed milk
200 g / 7 oz / 1 ⅓ cups dark
chocolate (minimum 60 %
cocoa solids), chopped
50 g / 1 ¾ oz / ½ cup butter

Method

1. Make the caramel layer in advance. Put the unopened can of condensed milk in a saucepan of water and simmer for 3 hours. Leave the can to cool completely.

2. Preheat the oven to 180°C (160°C fan) / 350F / gas 4 and line a 20 cm (8 in) square cake tin with greaseproof paper.

3. Mix together the flour and sugar in a bowl, then rub in the butter. Knead gently until the mixture forms a smooth dough, then press it into the bottom of the tin in an even layer.

4. Bake the shortbread for 20 minutes, turning the tray round halfway through. Leave to cool.

5. Open the can of condensed milk and beat the caramel until smooth. Spread it over the shortbread and chill for 1 hour.

6. Put the chocolate and butter in a bowl set over a pan of simmering water and stir together until melted and smooth.

7. Pour the mixture over the caramel layer and spread it out with a palette knife. Leave to set at room temperature before cutting into rectangles.

Carrot tray bake with orange cheesecake cream

Preparation time
30 minutes

Cooking time
40 minutes

Serves 10

Ingredients

175 g / 6 oz / 1 cup soft light brown sugar
2 large eggs
150 ml / 5 fl. oz / ⅔ cup sunflower oil
175 g / 6 oz / 1 ¼ cups plain (all-purpose) flour
3 tsp baking powder
2 tsp ground cinnamon
1 orange, zest finely grated
200 g / 7 oz / 1 ⅔ cups carrots, washed and coarsely grated

For the cream:
110 g / 4 oz / ½ cup cream cheese
55 g / 2 oz / ¼ cup butter, softened
110 g / 4 oz / 1 cup icing (confectioners') sugar
1 orange, juiced and zest finely grated

Method

1. Preheat the oven to 190°C (170°C fan) / 375F / gas 5 and line a 20 cm x 15 cm (8 in x 6 in) cake tin with greaseproof paper.

2. Whisk the sugar, eggs and oil together for 3 minutes until thick. Fold in the flour, baking powder and cinnamon, followed by the orange zest and carrots.

3. Scrape the mixture into the tin and bake for 40 minutes or until a skewer inserted comes out clean. Transfer the cake to a wire rack and leave to cool completely.

4. To make the cream, beat the cream cheese and butter together with a wooden spoon until light and fluffy, then beat in the icing sugar a quarter at a time. Stir in the orange zest and 2 tsp of juice, then use a whisk to whip the mixture for 2 minutes or until smooth and light.

5. Cut the cake into fingers and serve with a spoonful of the cheesecake cream.

Smart tip

If the cream is too stiff or too runny, adjust with a little more juice or sugar.

Smart tip

If the custard starts to bubble or rise in the oven, turn the temperature down by 10°C (50F).

Custard tart

Preparation time
45 minutes

Cooking time
55 minutes

Serves 8

Ingredients

100 g / 3 ½ oz / ½ cup butter,
  cubed
200 g / 7 oz / 1 ⅓ cups plain
  (all-purpose) flour
4 large egg yolks
75 g / 2 ½ oz / ⅓ cup caster
  (superfine) sugar
1 tsp vanilla extract
2 tsp cornflour (cornstarch)
450 ml / 16 fl. oz / 1 ¾ cups
  milk

Method

1. Preheat the oven to 200°C (180°C fan) / 390F / gas 6.

2. Rub the butter into the flour and add just enough cold water to bind. Chill the pastry for 30 minutes then roll out on a floured surface. Use the pastry to line a 23 cm (9 in) round tart case.

3. Prick the pastry with a fork, line with cling film and fill with baking beans or rice. Bake for 10 minutes, then remove the cling film and baking beans and cook for a further 8 minutes or until crisp.

4. Reduce the oven temperature to 160°C (140°C fan) / 325F / gas 3.

5. Whisk together the egg yolks, sugar, vanilla, cornflour and milk and strain it through a sieve into the pastry case.

6. Bake the tart for 35 minutes or until the custard is just set in the centre. Leave to cool completely before slicing.

Ginger loaf cake

Preparation time
15 minutes

Cooking time
40 minutes

Serves 10

Ingredients

250 g / 9 oz / 1 ⅔ cups
  self-raising flour
1 tsp bicarbonate of (baking)
  soda
2 tsp ground ginger
200 g / 8 ½ oz / ⅔ cup golden
  syrup
125 g / 4 ½ oz / ½ cup butter
125 g / 4 ½ oz / ¾ cup dark
  brown sugar
2 large eggs, beaten
250 ml / 9 fl. oz / 1 cup milk

Method

1. Preheat the oven to 180°C (160°C fan) / 355F / gas 4 and grease and line a loaf tin with greaseproof paper.
2. Sieve the flour, bicarbonate of soda and ginger into a bowl.
3. Put the golden syrup, butter and brown sugar in a small saucepan and boil gently for 2 minutes, stirring to dissolve the sugar.
4. Add the butter and sugar mixture to the flour with the eggs and milk and fold it all together until smooth.
5. Scrape the mixture into the prepared tin and bake for 40 minutes or until a skewer inserted comes out clean. Transfer the cake to a wire rack to cool completely before cutting and serving.

Smart tip

This moist cake will keep well for up to a week if stored in an airtight container.

Smart tip
Add the lemon juice to the buttercream gradually, stopping as soon as the right texture is reached.

Sultana sponge with lemon buttercream

Preparation time
45 minutes

Cooking time
35 minutes

Serves 10

Ingredients

200 g / 7 oz / 1 ⅓ cups
self-raising flour
200 g / 7 oz / ¾ cup caster
(superfine) sugar
200 g / 7 oz / ¾ cup butter,
softened
4 large eggs
1 tsp baking powder
75 g / 2 ½ oz / ⅓ cup sultanas

To decorate:
100 g / 3 ½ oz / ½ cup butter,
softened
200 g / 7 oz / 2 cups icing
(confectioners') sugar, plus
extra for dusting
½ lemon, juiced and zest
finely grated

Method

1. Preheat the oven to 180°C (160°C fan) / 350F / gas 4
   and grease and line two 20 cm (8 in) round loose-bottomed
   cake tins.

2. Put all of the cake ingredients in a large mixing bowl and
   whisk them together with an electric whisk for 4 minutes or
   until pale and well whipped. Divide the mixture between the
   two tins and level the tops with a spatula.

3. Bake for 35 minutes or until a toothpick inserted comes out
   clean. Transfer the cakes to a wire rack to cool completely.

4. To make the buttercream, whisk the butter with an electric
   whisk, then gradually add the icing sugar. Add the lemon
   zest and juice and whisk until smooth and well whipped.

5. Spoon the buttercream into a piping bag fitted with a large
   star nozzle and pipe the icing on top of one of the cakes.
   Position the other cake on top and dust with icing sugar.

Chocolate chip cookies

Preparation time
20 minutes

Cooking time
15 minutes

Serves 24

Ingredients

225 g / 8 oz / 1 ⅓ cups light
brown sugar
100 g / 3 ½ oz / ½ cup caster
(superfine) sugar
175 g / 6 oz / ¾ cup butter,
melted
2 tsp vanilla extract
1 egg, plus 1 egg yolk
250 g / 9 oz / 1 ⅔ cups
self-raising flour
100 g / 3 ½ oz / ⅔ cup dark
chocolate chips

Method

1. Preheat the oven to 160°C (140°C fan) / 325F / gas 3 and
   line two baking sheets with greaseproof paper.
2. Cream together the two sugars, butter and vanilla extract
   until pale and well whipped, then beat in the egg and yolk,
   followed by the flour and chocolate chips.
3. Use an ice cream scoop to portion the mixture onto the
   prepared trays, leaving plenty of room to spread.
4. Bake the cookies in batches for 15 minutes or until the
   edges are starting to brown, but the centres are still chewy.
   Transfer to a wire rack and leave to cool.

Smart tip

The biscuits will continue to harden as they cool, so try not to over cook them.

Smart tip

Don't make the scones
too thin or they'll be dry
when cooked.

Scones with jam and clotted cream

Preparation time
25 minutes

Cooking time
12 minutes

Serves 12

Ingredients

225 g / 8 oz / 1 ½ cups self-raising flour
55 g / 2 oz / ¼ cup butter
150 ml / 5 fl. oz / ⅔ cup whole (full-fat) milk
1 egg, beaten
200 g / 7 oz / ¾ cup clotted cream
200 g / 7 oz / ¾ cup raspberry jam (jelly)

Method

1. Preheat the oven to 220°C (200°C fan) / 425F / gas 7 and oil a large baking sheet.
2. Sieve the flour into a bowl and rub in the butter until the mixture resembles fine breadcrumbs.
3. Stir in enough milk to bring the mixture together into a soft dough.
4. Flatten the dough with your hands on a floured work surface until 2.5 cm (1 in) thick.
5. Use a pastry cutter to cut out 12 circles and transfer them to the prepared baking sheet, then brush with egg.
6. Bake in the oven for 12 minutes or until golden brown and cooked through. Transfer the scones to a wire rack to cool completely.
7. Split open the scones and top each half with clotted cream and raspberry jam.

Raspberry jam

Preparation time
5 minutes

Cooking time
40 minutes

Makes 700 ml

Ingredients

450 g / 1 lb / 2 cups
   granulated sugar
450 g / 1 lb / 3 cups
   raspberries
1 lemon, juiced

Method

1. Preheat the oven to 110°C (90°C fan) / 225F / gas ¼.
2. Put the sugar in a heatproof bowl and transfer it to the oven along with two glass jars to heat while you start cooking the fruit.
3. Put the raspberries and lemon juice in a large saucepan and cover with a lid. Heat gently for 10 minutes or until they simmer and soften in the juice they produce.
4. Stir in the warmed sugar to dissolve, then increase the heat and boil until the mixture reads 107°C / 225F on a sugar thermometer.
5. Leave the jam to cool and thicken for 10 minutes, then ladle into the prepared jars and seal with clean lids or waxed paper.

Smart tip

Only stir the jam occasionally or it will encourage the sugar to crystallise.

Smart tip
Infusing the pulp and
seeds in the juice
adds more pectin
for a better set.

Marmalade

Preparation time
30 minutes

Cooking time
1 hour 30 minutes

Makes 1 litre

Ingredients

550 g / 1 lb 3 ½ oz / 3 cups
  Seville oranges, halved
900 g / 2 lb / 4 cups
  granulated sugar

Method

1. Squeeze the juice from the oranges, reserving any pulp and seeds, then thinly slice the peel.

2. Put the reserved pulp and seeds in a muslin pouch and tie securely with string.

3. Put the orange juice, peel and muslin bag in a preserving pan with 2 litres / 4 ¼ pints / 8 ⅓ cups of water and leave to steep for 4 hours or overnight.

4. Once the contents have had chance to steep, put the preserving pan over a high heat and boil for 1 hour.

5. Preheat the oven to 110°C (90°C fan) / 225F / gas ¼ and put the sugar in a heatproof bowl inside along with three glass jars.

6. When the sugar has been in the oven for 10 minutes, squeeze out the muslin bag and discard, then stir the warmed sugar into the preserving pan until completely dissolved.

7. Skim off any scum that rises to the surface, then increase the heat and boil until a sugar thermometer reads 107°C / 225F.

8. Ladle the marmalade into the prepared jars while it's still hot, then seal with clean lids or waxed paper.

Pear and vanilla jam

Preparation time
5 minutes

Cooking time
40 minutes

Makes 1.2 litres

Ingredients

900 g / 2 lbs 5 / cups under-
  ripe pears
2 lemons, juiced
450 g / 1 lb / 2 cups
  granulated sugar
2 vanilla pods, split lengthways

Method

1. Preheat the oven to 110°C (90°C fan) / 225F / gas ¼ and put in four jars to sterilise.

2. Peel, core and dice the pears, then transfer them to a preserving pan, add the lemon juice and toss well.

3. Add the sugar and vanilla pods and stir well, then stir over a low heat until the sugar dissolves.

4. Increase the heat and boil until the mixture reads 107°C / 225F on a sugar thermometer.

5. Leave the jam to cool and thicken for 10 minutes, then ladle into the prepared jars and seal with clean lids or waxed paper.

Smart tip

Add the lemon juice to the pears as soon as possible after chopping to prevent them from going brown.

Smart tip

Macerating the fruit with the sugar overnight gets the juices flowing and the sugar dissolving.

Apricot and orange jam

Preparation time
4 hours

Cooking time
40 minutes

Makes 700 ml

Ingredients

450 g / 1 lb / 3 cups apricots,
  stoned and chopped
450 g / 1 lb / 2 cups
  granulated sugar
1 orange, zest finely pared

Method

1. Mix the apricots, sugar and orange zest together and leave to macerate for 4 hours or overnight.

2. When ready, transfer the mixture to a large saucepan and heat gently while stirring to dissolve the sugar.

3. Increase the heat and boil without stirring until the mixture reads 107°C / 225F on a sugar thermometer.

4. Leave the jam to cool and thicken for 10 minutes, then ladle into the sterilised jars and seal with clean lids or waxed paper.

Desserts

Treacle, date and oat puddings

Preparation time
25 minutes

Cooking time
25 minutes

Serves 8

Ingredients

250 g / 9 oz / 1 ⅔ cups
  self-raising flour
1 tsp bicarbonate of (baking)
  soda
100 g / 3 ½ oz / 1 cup rolled
  porridge oats
100 g / 3 ½ oz / ⅓ cup treacle
100 g / 3 ½ oz / ⅓ cup
  golden syrup
125 g / 4 ½ oz / ½ cup butter
125 g / 4 ½ oz / ¾ cup light
  brown sugar
125 g / 4 ½ oz / ⅔ cup
  medjool dates, stoned
  and quartered
2 large eggs, beaten
250 ml / 9 fl. oz / 1 cup milk

Method

1. Preheat the oven to 180°C (160°C fan) / 350F / gas 4 and butter eight individual baking dishes.

2. Sieve the flour and bicarbonate of soda into a bowl and stir in the oats.

3. Put the treacle, golden syrup, butter, brown sugar and dates in a small saucepan and boil gently for 2 minutes, stirring to dissolve the sugar.

4. Add the butter and sugar mixture to the flour with the eggs and milk and fold it all together until smooth.

5. Divide the mixture between the baking dishes and bake for 25 minutes or until a skewer inserted in the middle comes out with just a few damp crumbs sticking to it.

6. Serve hot from the oven.

Smart tip

Sit the baking dishes on a baking tray to make them easier to get in and out of the oven.

Smart tip

The uncooked crumble freezes really well – store in a freezer bag and defrost before baking.

Apple and cinnamon crumble

Preparation time
10 minutes

Cooking time
45 minutes

Serves 6

Ingredients

2 large cooking apples,
 peeled, cored and chopped
2 eating apples, peeled, cored
 and chopped
4 tbsp caster (superfine) sugar
75 g / 2 ½ oz / ⅓ cup butter
50 g / 1 ¾ oz / ⅓ cup plain
 (all-purpose) flour
25 g / 1 oz / ¼ cup ground
 almonds
2 tsp ground cinnamon
40 g / 1 ½ oz / ¼ cup light
 brown sugar

Method

1. Preheat the oven to 180°C (160°C fan) / 350F / gas 4.

2. Mix the apples with the sugar and arrange in a foil
   baking tray.

3. Rub the butter into the flour and stir in the ground almonds,
   cinnamon and brown sugar. Squeeze a handful of the
   mixture into a clump and then crumble it over the fruit.
   Use up the rest of the topping in the same way, then shake
   the dish to level the top.

4. Bake the crumble for 45 minutes or until the topping is
   golden brown.

Lemon meringue sponge

Preparation time
30 minutes

Cooking time
35 minutes

Serves 6

Ingredients

110 g / 4 oz / ⅔ cup
  self-raising flour, sifted
110 g / 4 oz / ½ cup caster
  (superfine) sugar
110 g / 4 oz / ½ cup butter,
  softened
2 large eggs
1 lemon, zest finely grated
225 g / 8 oz / 1 cup lemon
  curd

For the meringue:
4 large egg whites
110g / 4 oz / ½ cup caster
  (superfine) sugar

Method

1. Preheat the oven to 180°C (160°C fan) / 350F / gas 4 and oil and line a 23 cm (9 in) round cake tin with greaseproof paper.

2. Combine the flour, sugar, butter, eggs and lemon zest in a bowl and whisk together for 2 minutes or until smooth.

3. Scrape the mixture into the tin and level the top, then bake for 25 minutes or until a skewer inserted in the centre comes out clean.

4. Leave the sponge to cool for 10 minutes in the tin, then take it out, remove the greaseproof paper and transfer to a baking tray. Top the sponge with the lemon curd.

5. Whisk the egg whites until stiff, then gradually add the sugar and whisk until the mixture is thick and shiny. Spoon the meringue into a piping bag fitted with a large star nozzle and pipe it on top of the lemon curd.

6. Bake for 10 minutes or until golden brown.

Smart tip
This twist on the
classic pie is delicious
served warm with
pouring cream.

Smart tip

Baking the rice pudding at a low temperature gives it the best texture.

Sultana and marmalade rice pudding

Preparation time
5 minutes

Cooking time
1 hour 30 minutes

Serves 4

Ingredients

50 g / 1 ¾ oz / ¼ cup butter
110 g / 4 oz / ½ cup short
  grain rice
75 g / 2 ½ oz / ⅓ cup caster
  (superfine) sugar
75 g / 2 ½ oz / ⅓ cup golden
  sultanas
1 vanilla pod, seeds only
1.2 litres / 2 pints / 4 ½ cups
  whole (full-fat) milk
4 tbsp marmalade

Method

1. Preheat the oven to 140°C (120°C fan) / 275F / gas 1.
2. Melt the butter in a cast iron casserole dish and add the rice, sugar, sultanas and vanilla seeds.
3. Stir over a low heat for 2 minutes, then gradually incorporate the milk and bring to a simmer.
4. Cover the casserole dish and bake in the oven for 1 hour 30 minutes.
5. Stir in the marmalade and serve hot or chilled.

Apple sponge pudding

Preparation time
10 minutes

Cooking time
35 minutes

Serves 6

Ingredients

110 g / 4 oz / ⅔ cup
    self-raising flour, sifted
110 g / 4 oz / ½ cup light
    brown sugar
110 g / 4 oz / ½ cup butter,
    softened
2 large eggs
1 tsp ground ginger
1 tsp vanilla extract
2 dessert apples, cored
    and sliced
icing (confectioners') sugar for
    dusting

Method

1. Preheat the oven to 190°C (170°C fan) / 375F / gas 5 and
   butter a baking dish.

2. Combine the flour, sugar, butter, eggs, ground ginger and
   vanilla extract in a bowl and whisk together for 2 minutes or
   until smooth.

3. Scrape the mixture into the baking dish and arrange the
   apple slices on top.

4. Transfer the dish to the oven and bake for 35 minutes or
   until a skewer inserted comes out clean.

5. Serve the pudding hot from the oven, dusted with
   icing sugar.

Smart tip
This pudding is
delicious served with
cream or custard.

Smart tip

Sieve the flour before using for the best texture.

Lime and almond loaf cake

Preparation time
10 minutes

Cooking time
55 minutes

Serves 8

Ingredients

200 g / 7 oz / 1 ⅓ cups
  self-raising flour
50 g / 1 ¾ oz / ½ cup ground
  almonds
175 g / 6 oz / ¾ cup caster
  (superfine) sugar
175 g / 6 oz / ¾ cup butter,
  softened
3 large eggs
1 lime, juiced and zest
  finely grated
3 tbsp flaked (slivered)
  almonds

Method

1. Preheat the oven to 160°C (140°C fan) / 325F / gas 3 and line a large loaf tin with greaseproof paper.

2. Combine the flour, ground almonds, sugar, butter, eggs, 1 tbsp of lime juice and the lime zest in a bowl. Whisk together for 2 minutes or until smooth.

3. Scrape the mixture into the tin and level the top, then sprinkle with flaked almonds.

4. Bake for 55 minutes or until a skewer inserted comes out clean. Transfer to a wire rack and leave to cool completely before slicing.

Nut and caramel tart

Preparation time
1 hour

Cooking time
40 minutes

Serves 8

Ingredients

200 g / 7 oz / 1 ¼ cup light brown sugar
100 g / 3 ½ oz / ⅓ cup golden syrup
100 g / 3 ½ oz / ½ cup butter
1 tsp vanilla extract
3 large eggs, beaten
3 tbsp plain (all-purpose) flour
1 tsp mixed spice
300 g / 10 ½ oz / 1 ½ cups mixed nuts
3 tbsp dulce de leche

For the pastry:
150 g / 5 ½ oz / ⅔ cup butter, cubed and chilled
300 g / 10 ½ oz / 2 cups plain (all-purpose) flour

Method

1. First make the pastry. Rub the butter into the flour, then add just enough cold water to bind the mixture together into a pliable dough.

2. Roll out the pastry on a floured surface and use it to line a 23 cm (9 in) round tart case, then chill for 30 minutes.

3. Preheat the oven to 180°C (160°C fan) / 350F / gas 4.

4. Put the sugar, golden syrup, butter and vanilla extract in a saucepan and stir it over a low heat to dissolve the sugar. Leave the mixture to cool for 10 minutes, then beat in the eggs, flour and spice.

5. Pour the mixture into the pastry case and top with the nuts, then bake for 40 minutes.

6. As soon as the tart comes out of the oven, spoon over the dulce de leche and leave to cool for at least 15 minutes before cutting and serving.

Smart tip

The dulce de leche will melt over the tart in the residual heat to form a lovely glaze.

Strawberry trifles

Preparation time
35 minutes

Cooking time
10 minutes

Cooling time
1 hour

Serves 6

Ingredients

4 slices Madeira cake, cubed
4 tbsp sherry
200 g / 7 oz / 1 ⅓ cups
    strawberries, quartered
4 tbsp icing (confectioners')
    sugar
200 ml / 7 fl. oz / ¾ cup
    double (heavy) cream

For the custard:
450 ml / 12 ½ fl. oz / 1 ¾ cups
    whole (full-fat) milk
1 vanilla pod, split lengthways
4 large egg yolks
75 g / 2 ½ oz / ⅓ cup caster
    (superfine) sugar
1 tsp cornflour (cornstarch)

Method

1. Divide the cake between six sundae glasses and drizzle with sherry.

2. To make the custard, combine the milk and vanilla pod in a saucepan and bring to simmering point.

3. Meanwhile, whisk the egg yolks with the caster sugar and cornflour until thick.

4. Gradually incorporate the hot milk, whisking all the time, then scrape the mixture back into the saucepan.

5. Stir the custard over a low heat until it thickens, then spoon it into the glasses. Leave to cool to room temperature.

6. Purée half of the strawberries with the icing sugar in a liquidiser. Reserve a few strawberries for a garnish, then stir the rest into the purée and divide between the glasses.

7. Whip the cream until it forms soft peaks, then spoon it on top of the trifles and garnish with the reserved strawberries.

Pineapple tarte tatin

Preparation time
10 minutes

Cooking time
25 minutes

Serves 6

Ingredients

3 tbsp butter, softened and cubed
4 tbsp soft light brown sugar
400 g / 14 oz / 2 cups canned pineapple rings, drained
250 g / 9 oz / ¾ cup all-butter puff pastry

Method

1. Preheat the oven to 220°C (200°C fan) / 425F / gas 7.
2. Dot the butter over the base of a large ovenproof frying pan and sprinkle with sugar, then arrange the pineapple rings on top.
3. Roll out the pastry on a floured surface and cut out a circle the same size as the frying pan.
4. Lay the pastry over the fruit and tuck in the edges, then transfer the pan to the oven and bake for 25 minutes or until the pastry is golden brown and cooked through.
5. Using oven gloves, put a large plate on top of the frying pan and turn them both over in one smooth movement to unmould the tart.

Smart tip

Arrange the pineapple rings in a single layer, cutting up any that won't fit and tucking them in between.

Smart tip

Cooling the meringues slowly inside the oven stops them from cracking.

Individual strawberry pavlovas

Preparation time
1 hour 30 minutes

Cooking time
1 hour

Makes 4

Ingredients

4 large egg whites
110 g / 4 oz / 1 cup caster
  (superfine) sugar
1 tsp cornflour (cornstarch)
225 ml / 8 fl. oz / ¾ cup
  double (heavy) cream
2 tbsp icing (confectioners')
  sugar
½ tsp vanilla extract
150 g / 5 ½ oz / 1 cup
  strawberries, halved
4 tbsp strawberry syrup

Method

1. Preheat the oven to 140°C (120°C fan) / 275F / gas 1 and oil
   and line a baking tray with greaseproof paper.

2. Whisk the egg whites until stiff, then gradually whisk in
   half the sugar until the mixture is very shiny. Fold in the
   remaining sugar and the cornflour, then spoon the mixture
   into four mounds on the baking tray.

3. Bake the meringues for 1 hour or until they lift easily off the
   baking paper and sound hollow when tapped. Turn off the
   oven and leave the meringues to cool completely inside.

4. Whip the cream with the icing sugar and vanilla until it just
   holds its shape, then spoon it on top of the meringues.
   Arrange the strawberries on top and drizzle with
   strawberry syrup.

Spiced pear tart

Preparation time
20 minutes

Cooking time
30 minutes

Serves 6

Ingredients

450 g / 1 lb / 1 ½ cups ready-
  to-roll puff pastry
75 g / 2 ½ oz / ¾ cup ground
  almonds
75 g / 2 ½ oz / ⅓ cup butter,
  softened
75 g / 2 ½ oz / ⅓ cup dark
  muscovado sugar
1 large egg
2 tsp mixed spice
1 tbsp plain (all-purpose) flour
50 g / 1 ¾ oz / 1 cup amaretti
  biscuits, crushed
3 pears, peeled, cored
  and sliced

Method

1. Preheat the oven to 200°C (180°C fan) / 400F / gas 6.

2. Roll out the pastry on a floured surface into a large circle, then transfer to a lined baking tray.

3. Whisk together the almonds, butter, sugar, eggs, spice and flour until smoothly whipped, then fold in two thirds of the crushed biscuits.

4. Spread the mixture on top of the pastry, leaving a 2.5 cm (1 in) border round the outside.

5. Arrange the pear halves on top, then sprinkle with the rest of the amaretti biscuits and fold in the edges of the pastry.

6. Bake the tart for 30 minutes or until cooked through in the centre.

Smart tip

Make sure all of the pear slices are the same thickness so that they cook evenly.

Smart tip

You can buy the
chocolate curls from
cake decorating shops
or online.

Moist chocolate flower cake

Preparation time
45 minutes

Cooking time
40 minutes

Serves 8

Ingredients

250 g / 9 oz / 1 ⅔ cups
  self-raising flour
1 tsp bicarbonate of (baking)
  soda
4 tbsp unsweetened cocoa
  powder
200 g / 8 ½ oz / ⅔ cup golden
  syrup
125 g / 4 ½ oz / ½ cup butter
125 g / 4 ½ oz / ¾ cup dark
  brown sugar
2 large eggs, beaten
250 ml / 9 fl. oz / 1 cup milk
4 tbsp chocolate syrup
3 tbsp dark chocolate curls
3 tbsp white chocolate curls
icing (confectioners') sugar for
  dusting

Method

1. Preheat the oven to 180°C (160°C fan) / 350F / gas 4 and grease and line a flower-shaped cake tin.

2. Sieve the flour, bicarbonate of soda and cocoa into a bowl.

3. Put the golden syrup, butter and brown sugar in a small saucepan and boil gently for 2 minutes, stirring to dissolve the sugar.

4. Add the butter and sugar mixture to the flour with the eggs and milk and fold it all together until smooth.

5. Scrape the mixture into the prepared tin and bake for 40 minutes or until a skewer inserted in the centre comes out clean. Pierce the cake all over with a skewer and drizzle over the chocolate syrup, then leave to cool completely before unmoulding.

6. Transfer the cake to a cake stand and top with the chocolate curls and a dusting of icing sugar.

Apricot frangipane tart

Preparation time
30 minutes

Cooking time
35 minutes

Serves 8

Ingredients

450 g / 1 lb / 1 ½ cups puff
pastry
225 g / 8 oz / 2 ¼ cups
ground almonds
225 g / 8 oz / 1 cup butter,
softened
225 g / 8 oz / 1 cup caster
(superfine) sugar
3 large eggs
1 tsp almond extract
3 tbsp plain (all-purpose) flour
12 apricots, stoned and halved

Method

1. Preheat the oven to 200°C (180°C fan) / 400F / gas 6 and
   line a large rectangular tart case with greaseproof paper.

2. Roll out the pastry on a floured surface and use it to line the
   tart case.

3. Prick the pastry with a fork, line with greaseproof paper and
   fill with baking beans or rice.

4. Bake for 10 minutes, then remove the paper and baking
   beans and leave to cool.

5. Whisk together the almonds, butter, sugar, eggs, almond
   extract and flour until smoothly whipped, then spoon the
   mixture into the pastry case.

6. Press the apricots into the frangipane, cut side down and
   bake the tart for 25 minutes or until the frangipane is cooked
   through and the pastry is crisp underneath.

Smart tip

Tiny air bubbles in the meringue act as an insulator for the ice cream, but the Alaska must be completely sealed for this to work.

Toffee baked Alaska

Preparation time
45 minutes

Cooking time
25 minutes

Freezing time
2 hours

Serves 8

Ingredients

55 g / 2 oz / ⅓ cup self-raising
flour, sifted
55 g / 2 oz / ¼ cup caster
(superfine) sugar
55 g / 1 oz / ¼ cup butter,
softened
1 large egg
½ tsp vanilla extract
750 ml / 1 pint 5 ½ fl. oz /
3 cups vanilla ice cream,
softened
225 g / 8 oz / 1 cup dulce de
leche
4 large egg whites
110g / 4 oz / ½ cup caster
(superfine) sugar

Method

1. Preheat the oven to 180°C (160°C fan) / 350F / gas 4 and
oil and line a 26 cm (10 in) straight-sided loaf tin with
greaseproof paper.

2. Combine the flour, sugar, butter, egg and vanilla extract in a
bowl and whisk together for 2 minutes or until smooth.

3. Scrape the mixture into the tin and level the top, then bake
for 15 minutes or until a skewer inserted in the centre comes
out clean.

4. Leave to cool completely, then remove from the tin. Line the
tin with cling film and put the cake back in the bottom. Top
with half of the ice cream and smooth into an even layer.

5. Spoon half of the dulce de leche on top, then add another
layer of ice cream, followed by the rest of the dulce de leche.

6. Transfer the tin to the freezer and freeze for 2 hours or
until solid.

7. Whisk the egg whites until stiff, then gradually add the sugar
and whisk until the mixture is thick and shiny. Spoon the
meringue into a piping bag fitted with a large star nozzle.

8. Preheat the oven to 230°C (210°C fan) / 450F / gas 8.
Unmould the Alaska and transfer it to a baking tray,
discarding the cling film. Pipe the meringue over the top
and sides, ensuring it is completely covered with no gaps.

9. Bake for 10 minutes or until golden brown, then
serve immediately.

Gluten-free nectarine sponge

Preparation time
10 minutes

Cooking time
30 minutes

Serves 6

Ingredients

110 g / 4 oz / ⅔ cup gluten-free self-raising flour, sifted
110 g / 4 oz / ½ cup caster (superfine) sugar
110 g / 4 oz / ½ cup butter, softened
2 large eggs
1 tsp almond extract
3 small nectarines, stoned and sliced

Method

1. Preheat the oven to 190°C (170°C fan) / 375F / gas 5 and butter a round tart tin.

2. Combine the flour, sugar, butter, eggs and almond extract in a bowl and whisk together for 2 minutes or until smooth.

3. Scrape the mixture into the baking dish and arrange the nectarine slices on top.

4. Transfer the tin to the oven and bake for 30 minutes or until a skewer inserted comes out clean. Leave to cool completely in the tin before cutting and serving.

Smart tip

Don't use a loose-bottomed tart tin as the cake mixture may run through.

Smart tip

Don't miss out the chilling stage as it is vital for getting the right texture.

Milk chocolate fondants

Preparation time
50 minutes

Cooking time
8 minutes

Makes 6

Ingredients

2 tbsp unsweetened cocoa
   powder
150 g / 6 oz / 1 cup good-
   quality milk chocolate,
   chopped
150 g / 6 oz / ⅔ cup butter,
   chopped
85 g / 3 oz / ½ cup caster
   (superfine) sugar
3 large eggs, plus 3 egg yolks
1 tbsp plain (all-purpose) flour
icing (confectioners') sugar
   for dusting

Method

1. Butter six mini casserole dishes and dust the insides with cocoa.

2. Melt the chocolate, butter and sugar together in a saucepan, stirring to dissolve the sugar. Leave to cool a little, then beat in the eggs and egg yolks and fold in the flour.

3. Divide the mixture between the dishes and chill for 30 minutes.

4. Preheat the oven to 180°C (160°C fan) / 350F / gas 4 and put a baking tray in to heat.

5. Transfer the fondants to the heated baking tray and bake in the oven for 8 minutes.

6. Leave the fondants to cool for 2 minutes, then sprinkle with icing sugar and serve immediately.

Sultana bread and butter pudding

Preparation time
45 minutes

Cooking time
40 minutes

Serves 4

Ingredients

1 loaf white bread, sliced and
  crusts removed
3 tbsp butter, softened
100 g / 3 ½ oz / ⅔ cup sultanas
250 ml / 9 fl. oz / 1 cup whole
  (full-fat) milk
200 ml / 7 fl. oz / ¾ cup
  double (heavy) cream
4 large egg yolks
75 g / 2 ½ oz / ⅓ cup caster
  (superfine) sugar

Method

1. Spread the bread with butter and cut it into quarters.
2. Arrange the squares in a baking dish, sprinkling in the sultanas as you go.
3. Whisk the milk, cream, eggs and caster sugar together and pour it over the top, then leave to soak for 30 minutes.
4. Preheat the oven to 180°C (160°C fan) / 350F / gas 4.
5. Bake the pudding for 40 minutes or until the top is golden brown.

Smart tip

Make sure you butter
the bread slices right
up to the edges so they
don't go dry in
the oven.

Index

Shepherd's pie with leeks, *114*
Smoked fish casserole, *134*
Smoked haddock chowder, *61*

Potatoes, sweet
Sweet potato and carrot soup, *41*

Prosciutto
Eggs Benedict, *28*
Ham and pea pasta bake, *122*

Pumpkin
Pumpkin soup with Parmesan tuiles, *62*

Quinoa
Quinoa granola with fromage frais, *16*

Radishes
Chicken, apple and red cabbage salad, *73*

Ras el hanout spice mix
Lamb, pepper and fig tagine, *130*

Raspberries
Raspberry jam, *176*

Rice
Pork, rice and vegetable stew, *141*
Rice salad Niçoise, *69*
Sultana and marmalade rice pudding, *193*

Rocket (arugula)
Courgette, ham and mini mozzarella salad, *78*

Salmon
Salmon en croûte, *113*

Salmon, smoked
Individual smoked salmon quiches, *93*

Sausages
Baked mushrooms with sausage scramble, *8*
Fettuccini with walnut meatballs, *98*
Full English breakfast, *15*
Meatloaf with roasted carrots, *102*
Stuffed round courgettes, *90*

Scallops
Scallop and leek stew, *138*

Shallots
Chicken and kale cannelloni, *106*
Eggs Benedict, *28*

Sherry
Strawberry trifles, *201*

Spinach
Chicken, potato and flageolet bean stew, *149*
Rice salad Niçoise, *69*

Sprouting seeds
Tomato and mozzarella salad with sprouting seeds, *66*

Star anise
Turkey, parsnip and Irish stout casserole, *153*

Strawberries
Fruit salad with strawberry sauce, *20*
Individual strawberry pavlovas, *205*
Strawberry trifles, *201*

Stout, Irish
Turkey, parsnip and Irish stout casserole, *153*

Sultanas
Sultana and marmalade rice pudding, *193*
Sultana bread and butter pudding, *218*
Sultana sponge with lemon buttercream, *171*

Swede
Root vegetable soup, *49*

Tomatoes
Beef and Red Leicester bagel, *86*
Chickpea, lentil and cabbage salad, *70*
Chunky beef chilli, *146*
Courgette, ham and mini mozzarella salad, *78*
Fettuccini with walnut meatballs, *98*
Full English breakfast, *15*
Greek salad, *77*
Lasagne, *118*
Mediterranean vegetable stew, *150*
Rice salad Niçoise, *69*
Tomato and mozzarella salad with sprouting seeds, *66*
Tomato and thyme soup, *38*
Vegetable moussaka, *105*

Tomato passata
Chicken, potato and flageolet bean stew, *149*

Tomato pizza sauce
Ham and mushroom pizza, *125*

Tomato purée
Fish soup, *53*

Treacle
Treacle, date and oat puddings, *186*

Tuna
Rice salad Niçoise, *69*

Turkey
Maple-roasted turkey breast with bread sauce, *94*
Meatloaf with roasted carrots, *102*
Stuffed round courgettes, *90*
Turkey, parsnip and Irish stout casserole, *153*

Vanilla
Apple sponge pudding, *194*
Chocolate chip cookies, *172*
Custard tart, *167*
Individual strawberry pavlovas, *205*
Nut and caramel tart, *198*
Pear and vanilla jam, *180*

Strawberry Swiss roll, *160*
Strawberry trifles, *201*
Sultana and marmalade rice pudding, *193*
Toffee baked Alaska, *213*

Veal
Creamy veal and wild mushroom casserole, *137*
Veal Caesar salad, *74*

Vinegar, balsamic
Tomato and mozzarella salad with sprouting seeds, *66*

Vinegar, white wine
Eggs Benedict, *28*

Walnuts
Fettuccini with walnut meatballs, *98*

Watercress
Watercress and mushroom soup, *46*

Wild garlic leaves
Mini casserole of cod with wild garlic pesto, *154*

Wine, red
Coq au vin, *142*

Wine, white
Braised lamb shanks with carrots, *110*
Lamb and carrot lattice pie, *85*
Scallop and leek stew, *138*

Yeast, easy-blend
Crumpets, *24*
Danish pastries, *31*
Ham and mushroom pizza, *125*